LEADERSHIP IN DIGITAL ERA

NAVIGATE CHANGE
AND
DRIVE INNOVATION

BY AHMAD MANZOOR

This book is dedicated to all the wonderful leaders of past, present & future.

Ahmad Manzoor
http://www.ahmadmanzoor.net

Table of Content

Conclusion:

PROLOGUE

In today's fast-paced world, digital technology has transformed the way we work and live. From social media to artificial intelligence, technology has reshaped how we communicate, consume information, and make decisions. In this context, leadership has become more important than ever before. Effective leaders must be able to navigate change and drive innovation in order to stay competitive in a rapidly evolving landscape.

The book "Leadership in the Digital Age: Navigate Change and Drive Innovation" is a guide for leaders who want to thrive in this new era. It provides practical strategies and tools for navigating the complexities of digital transformation and leveraging technology to drive innovation. From developing a digital mindset to fostering a culture of experimentation, the book offers insights from experts in the field and real-world examples of successful digital leadership.

Whether you are a CEO, manager, or entrepreneur, "Leadership in the Digital Age" will help you stay ahead of the curve and lead your organization to success in a constantly evolving digital landscape. With its actionable insights and compelling case studies, this book is a must-read for anyone who wants to stay competitive and drive innovation in the digital age.

X.
INTRODUCTION

The digital age has brought about a wave of disruption and change that has transformed the way we live, work, and do business. As technology continues to advance at an unprecedented pace, leaders are faced with the challenge of navigating this rapidly changing landscape and driving innovation in their organizations.

In this chapter, we will explore the concept of digital transformation and the importance of digital leadership in the modern business environment. We will also introduce the key themes and topics that will be covered throughout the book.

Digital Transformation

The first section of this chapter will define digital transformation and explore the ways in which it is reshaping the business landscape. We will discuss the impact of digital technologies on consumer behavior, business operations, and industry structures.

The Role of Leadership in Digital Transformation

The second section of this chapter will highlight the critical role that leadership plays in driving digital transformation. We will explore the characteristics of effective digital leaders and discuss the importance of vision, innovation, and collaboration.

The Structure of the Book

The final section of this chapter will provide an overview of the structure of the book. We will introduce the four parts of the book, which include building a culture of innovation, leading change in a digital world, preparing for the future of digital leadership, and the conclusion.

Overall, this chapter sets the stage for the rest of the book and highlights the importance of digital leadership in the face of ongoing digital transformation. It provides readers with a framework for understanding the challenges and opportunities presented by the digital age and prepares them for the practical strategies and techniques that will be presented throughout the book.

Digital Transformation

In recent years, the digital age has brought about a fundamental transformation in the way that we live, work, and do business. The widespread adoption of digital technologies, including cloud computing, artificial intelligence, and the Internet of Things, has led to the creation of new business models, products, and services. Digital transformation refers to the process of using digital technologies to fundamentally change the way that businesses operate and deliver value to customers. This transformation can involve the adoption of new technologies, the rethinking of business processes, and the development of new business models.

The impact of digital transformation on consumer behavior has been significant. Consumers have come to expect fast, convenient, and personalized experiences across all channels and touchpoints. Businesses that are unable to meet these expectations risk losing customers to more agile and digitally savvy competitors.

In addition to changing consumer behavior, digital transformation has also led to the reorganization of traditional industry structures. New entrants, unencumbered by legacy systems and processes, have disrupted established industries and created new markets.

In order to remain competitive in the digital age, businesses must embrace digital transformation and adapt to the changing landscape. This requires strong leadership and a willingness to embrace change and innovation. In the following sections of the book, we will explore the key principles and strategies that underpin effective digital leadership and help organizations navigate the ongoing process of digital transformation.

The Role of Leadership in Digital Transformation

Leadership plays a critical role in driving digital transformation in organizations. Digital leaders must have a clear vision of where they want to take their organizations and the ability to inspire and motivate their teams to achieve that vision.

Effective digital leaders are also innovative and able to identify and leverage emerging technologies to create new opportunities for their organizations. They are comfortable with uncertainty and ambiguity and are willing to take calculated risks in order to drive innovation.

In addition to vision and innovation, collaboration is also essential to effective digital leadership. Digital leaders must be able to bring together diverse teams and stakeholders and foster a culture of collaboration and experimentation.

Furthermore, effective digital leaders are also adept at managing change. They must be able to anticipate and respond to the challenges and opportunities presented by digital transformation and navigate their organizations through periods of uncertainty and disruption.

To succeed in the digital age, organizations must cultivate a culture of digital leadership at all levels. This requires investing in the development of digital leadership skills and fostering a culture of continuous learning and experimentation.

In the following sections of the book, we will explore the practical strategies and techniques that digital leaders can use to build a culture of innovation, lead change in a digital world, and prepare for the future of digital leadership. By embracing digital leadership, organizations can drive innovation, navigate change, and thrive in the fast-paced and constantly evolving digital landscape.

The Structure of this Book

This book is divided into four parts, each of which explores a different aspect of digital leadership and provides practical guidance and strategies for navigating the challenges and opportunities presented by digital transformation.

Part I: Understanding the Digital Landscape of "Leadership in the Digital Age" focuses on helping readers understand the digital landscape and the impact of digital transformation on modern leadership.

"Chapter 1: The Impact of Digital Transformation on Leadership" sets the stage by introducing the concept of digital transformation and exploring how it has changed the business landscape. The chapter highlights the challenges and opportunities that digital transformation presents for leaders and provides insights into how to navigate this new reality.

Introduction to digital transformation and its impact on modern leadership
Understanding the ways in which technology has changed the business landscape
The challenges and opportunities presented by digital transformation for leaders

"Chapter 2: Navigating the Technological Landscape: Key Trends and Tools" provides an overview of the most important technological trends and tools leaders need to be aware of. This chapter explores emerging technologies such as AI, machine learning, and blockchain and their potential impact on different industries. It helps readers understand the potential of these technologies and how to leverage them to drive innovation and growth.

The most important technological trends and tools leaders need to be aware of
An overview of emerging technologies such as AI, machine learning, and blockchain
Understanding the potential impact of these technologies on different industries

"Chapter 3: The Role of Data in Modern Leadership" focuses on the role of data in modern leadership. This chapter highlights the importance of data in driving business decisions and explores the types of data available and how to use them effectively. It provides strategies for collecting, analyzing, and using data to drive innovation and growth.

Overall, Part I provides readers with a solid foundation for understanding the digital landscape and the impact of digital transformation on modern leadership. It sets the stage for the rest of the book and prepares readers for the practical strategies and techniques presented in subsequent chapters.

The importance of data in driving business decisions
Understanding the types of data available and how to use them effectively
Strategies for collecting, analyzing, and using data to drive innovation and growth

Part II: Building a Culture of Innovation of "Leadership in the Digital Age" focuses on building a culture of innovation in the digital age.

"Chapter 4: Creating a Culture of Innovation: Principles and Practices" defines innovation and explores its importance in modern business. It helps readers understand the elements of a culture of innovation and how to build a culture of innovation in their organization.

Defining innovation and its importance in modern business
Understanding the elements of a culture of innovation
How to build a culture of innovation in your organization

"Chapter 5: Empowering and Encouraging Creativity: Strategies for Success" emphasizes the importance of creativity in innovation and provides strategies for encouraging and fostering creativity in your team. It highlights the value of empowering employees to take ownership of their ideas and innovations.

The importance of creativity in innovation
How to encourage and foster creativity in your team
Strategies for empowering employees to take ownership of their ideas and innovations

"Chapter 6: The Importance of Failure: Learning from Setbacks and Mistakes" explores the role of failure in the innovation process and provides strategies for embracing and learning from failures and setbacks. It helps readers create a culture that encourages risk-taking and experimentation.

The role of failure in the innovation process
Strategies for embracing and learning from failures and setbacks
How to create a culture that encourages risk-taking and experimentation

Overall, Part II provides readers with practical strategies and techniques for building a culture of innovation. It emphasizes the importance of creativity, risk-taking, and experimentation and prepares readers for leading change in the digital age.

Part III: Leading Change in a Digital World of "Leadership in the Digital Age" focuses on leading change in a digital world.

"Chapter 7: Leading Change: The Importance of Vision and Communication" highlights the role of leaders in driving change and provides strategies for creating a compelling vision for change. It explores how to communicate change effectively to your team and the importance of vision and communication.

The role of leaders in driving change
How to create a compelling vision for change
Strategies for communicating change effectively to your team

"Chapter 8: Overcoming Resistance to Change: Strategies and Techniques" addresses common sources of resistance to change and provides strategies for overcoming them. It helps readers engage employees and stakeholders in the change process and create a sense of urgency and momentum for change.

Common sources of resistance to change and how to overcome them
Strategies for engaging employees and stakeholders in the change process
How to create a sense of urgency and build momentum for change

"Chapter 9: Building Agile Teams: Adapting to Rapidly Changing Circumstances" focuses on building agile teams that can adapt quickly to change. It explores the importance of agility in a rapidly changing business environment and provides strategies for creating a culture that encourages flexibility and innovation in the face of change.

The importance of agility in a rapidly changing business environment
Strategies for building agile teams that can adapt quickly to change
How to create a culture that encourages flexibility and innovation in the face of change

Overall, Part III helps readers understand the importance of leadership in driving change in a digital world. It provides practical strategies and techniques for overcoming resistance to change and building agile teams that can adapt to rapidly changing circumstances. Part III prepares readers for the future of digital leadership.

Part IV: The Future of Digital Leadership of "Leadership in the Digital Age" focuses on the future of digital leadership and how to prepare for disruptive changes.

"Chapter 10: Emerging Technologies and Their Implications for Leadership" provides an overview of emerging technologies that are likely to shape the future of business. It explores the potential impact of these technologies on leadership and management and provides strategies for staying up-to-date and adapting to new technologies.

An overview of emerging technologies that are likely to shape the future of business
The potential impact of these technologies on leadership and management

Strategies for staying up-to-date and adapting to new technologies

"Chapter 11: The Future of Work: Preparing for Disruptive Changes" explores the impact of technology on the future of work. It helps readers understand the trends that are likely to shape the future of work and provides strategies for preparing for and adapting to disruptive changes in the workplace.

The impact of technology on the future of work
Understanding the trends that are likely to shape the future of work
Strategies for preparing for and adapting to disruptive changes in the workplace

"Chapter 12: The Ethics of Digital Leadership: Balancing Profit and Social Responsibility" focuses on the importance of ethical leadership in a digital world. It explores the ethical challenges presented by emerging technologies and provides strategies for balancing profit and social responsibility in the digital age.

The importance of ethical leadership in a digital world
Understanding the ethical challenges presented by emerging technologies
Strategies for balancing profit and social responsibility in the digital age

Overall, Part IV helps readers prepare for the future of digital leadership. It explores emerging technologies, the future of work, and the importance of ethical leadership. It provides strategies for staying up-to-date and adapting to disruptive changes and encourages readers to develop a personalized approach to digital leadership. Part IV prepares readers to navigate the rapidly changing digital landscape and lead their organizations to success.

The conclusion of "Leadership in the Digital Age" brings together the key themes and takeaways from the book. It emphasizes the importance of digital transformation, building a culture of innovation, leading change, and preparing for the future of digital leadership.

The conclusion encourages readers to take action and apply the practical strategies and techniques presented in the book. It highlights the importance of continuous learning and adaptation in the rapidly changing digital landscape.

The conclusion also acknowledges that digital leadership is a journey and that there is no one-size-fits-all approach. It encourages readers to develop their own personalized approach to digital leadership and to experiment, learn, and adapt as they go.

Overall, the conclusion of the book provides a final call to action and encourages readers to embrace digital leadership and drive innovation in their organizations. It leaves readers with a sense of inspiration and confidence to navigate the challenges and opportunities presented by the digital age.

Recap of the key themes and lessons from the book

Strategies for developing a personalized approach to digital leadership

Encouragement to continue learning and adapting in the rapidly changing digital landscape.

1.

THE IMPACT OF DIGITAL TRANSFORMATION ON LEADERSHIP

In today's rapidly evolving digital landscape, digital transformation has become a critical imperative for organizations seeking to remain competitive and relevant. However, the process of digital transformation also presents significant challenges for leaders, requiring them to adapt to new technologies, changing business models, and evolving customer expectations. In this chapter, we will explore the impact of digital transformation on leadership and the key competencies required of digital leaders in the digital age.

The Digital Landscape

The first section of the chapter provides an overview of the digital landscape and the key trends and technologies driving digital transformation. We will examine the role of technologies such as artificial intelligence, cloud computing, and the internet of things in transforming business models and creating new opportunities for innovation and growth.

The Challenges of Digital Transformation for Leaders

The second section of the chapter focuses on the challenges of digital transformation for leaders. We will explore the ways in which digital transformation is disrupting traditional business models and creating new challenges for leaders, including the need to adapt to new technologies, the need to create a culture of innovation and experimentation, and the need to navigate uncertainty and ambiguity.

The Competencies of Digital Leaders

The third section of the chapter explores the competencies required of digital leaders in the digital age. We will examine the key skills and attributes that digital leaders must possess, including the ability to inspire and motivate their teams, the ability to innovate and create new opportunities, and the ability to navigate change and uncertainty.

The Benefits of Digital Leadership

The final section of the chapter examines the benefits of digital leadership for organizations. We will explore the ways in which effective digital leadership can drive innovation, create new opportunities for growth, and enable organizations to remain competitive in a rapidly evolving digital landscape.

Conclusion

In conclusion, the impact of digital transformation on leadership is significant, requiring leaders to adapt to new technologies, create a culture of innovation, and navigate uncertainty and ambiguity. However, by embracing digital leadership and developing the key competencies required to succeed in the digital age, organizations can drive innovation, navigate change, and remain competitive in the fast-paced and constantly evolving digital landscape.

The Digital Landscape

The digital landscape is constantly evolving, driven by emerging technologies and changing customer expectations. Digital transformation has become a critical imperative for organizations seeking to remain competitive and relevant, as it presents new opportunities for innovation and growth while also creating new challenges for leaders.

One of the key drivers of digital transformation is the proliferation of data and the rise of artificial intelligence (AI) and machine learning (ML) technologies. These technologies are enabling organizations to analyze vast amounts of data and derive insights that can be used to inform business decisions and drive innovation. They are also enabling organizations to automate routine tasks and streamline operations, freeing up resources to focus on more strategic initiatives.

Another key driver of digital transformation is the growth of cloud computing and the shift towards software-as-a-service (SaaS) models. Cloud computing has made it easier and more cost-effective for organizations to adopt new technologies and scale their operations, while SaaS models are enabling organizations to access powerful software tools without the need for significant up-front investments.

The Internet of Things (IoT) is also playing a key role in driving digital transformation, as it enables organizations to collect and analyze data from a wide range of sources, including sensors and other connected devices. This data can be used to optimize operations, improve customer experiences, and create new opportunities for innovation and growth.

Overall, the digital landscape is rapidly evolving, creating both opportunities and challenges for organizations and their leaders. To succeed in the digital age, leaders must be able to adapt to new technologies and business models, embrace a culture of innovation, and navigate the uncertainties and complexities of the digital landscape.

The Challenges of Digital Transformation for Leaders

Digital transformation presents a number of challenges for leaders, requiring them to adapt to new technologies and business models while also navigating the uncertainties and complexities of the digital landscape. Some of the key challenges of digital transformation for leaders include the following:

Adapting to new technologies: Digital transformation is often driven by emerging technologies such as AI, ML, and IoT, which can be complex and difficult to implement. Leaders must be able to understand these technologies and their implications for their organization, as well as identify the right tools and platforms to leverage.

Creating a culture of innovation: Digital transformation requires organizations to be innovative and agile in their approach, constantly experimenting and iterating to find new ways of delivering value to customers. Leaders must be able to create a culture of innovation within their organization, fostering creativity and empowering their teams to take risks and explore new ideas.

Navigating uncertainty and ambiguity: The digital landscape is constantly evolving, creating uncertainty and ambiguity for organizations and their leaders. Leaders must be able to navigate this uncertainty, making strategic decisions based on incomplete information and adapting quickly to changing circumstances.

Managing digital talent: Digital transformation requires a skilled workforce that is able to leverage new technologies and drive innovation. Leaders must be able to attract and retain digital talent, providing them with the training and support they need to succeed in the digital age.

Ensuring cybersecurity: As organizations become increasingly reliant on digital technologies, cybersecurity becomes a critical concern. Leaders must be able to ensure that their organization's digital assets are secure, protecting against cyber threats and data breaches.

Overall, the challenges of digital transformation for leaders are significant, requiring them to be adaptable, innovative, and agile in their approach. To succeed in the digital age, leaders must be able to navigate uncertainty and complexity, embrace a culture of innovation, and leverage emerging technologies to drive growth and create value for customers.

The Opportunities of Digital Transformation for Leaders

While digital transformation presents significant challenges for leaders, it also presents a range of opportunities, enabling organizations to innovate and grow in new and exciting ways. Some of the key opportunities of digital transformation for leaders include the following:

Enhancing customer experiences: Digital technologies enable organizations to personalize and customize their products and services to meet the unique needs and preferences of individual customers. Leaders can leverage data and analytics to gain insights into customer behavior, enabling them to deliver more personalized and engaging experiences.

Streamlining operations: Digital technologies can be used to automate routine tasks and streamline operations, reducing costs and improving efficiency. Leaders can leverage technologies such as robotic process automation (RPA) and workflow automation to optimize business processes and improve productivity.

Enabling new business models: Digital technologies are enabling organizations to create new business models and revenue streams. For example, organizations can leverage the sharing economy model to create new opportunities for collaboration and innovation, or create new digital products and services that leverage emerging technologies such as blockchain and AI.

Improving decision-making: Digital technologies enable organizations to collect and analyze vast amounts of data, providing leaders with real-time insights into business performance and customer behavior. Leaders can leverage this data to make more informed decisions, improving the overall effectiveness and efficiency of their organization.

Empowering employees: Digital technologies enable organizations to provide their employees with new tools and platforms to collaborate, communicate, and innovate. Leaders can leverage these technologies to create a more agile and flexible workforce, empowering their employees to work more effectively and creatively.

Overall, the opportunities of digital transformation for leaders are significant, enabling organizations to innovate and grow in new and exciting ways. By leveraging emerging technologies and adopting a culture of innovation, leaders can create value for their customers and drive growth and success in the digital age.

Strategies for Leaders to Navigate Digital Transformation

To successfully navigate digital transformation, leaders must adopt a range of strategies that enable them to address the challenges and opportunities of the digital age. Some key strategies for leaders to navigate digital transformation include the following:

Develop a digital strategy: Leaders must develop a clear digital strategy that aligns with the overall goals and objectives of their organization. This strategy should outline how digital technologies will be used to create value for customers, improve business processes, and drive growth and innovation.

Foster a culture of innovation: To succeed in the digital age, organizations must be innovative and agile in their approach. Leaders must foster a culture of innovation within their organization, encouraging experimentation, risk-taking, and creativity.

Invest in digital talent: Digital transformation requires a skilled workforce that is able to leverage emerging technologies and drive innovation. Leaders must invest in digital talent, providing employees with the training and support they need to succeed in the digital age.

Embrace emerging technologies: Leaders must be open to exploring emerging technologies such as AI, blockchain, and the Internet of Things (IoT), identifying opportunities to leverage these technologies to create value for customers and improve business processes.

Foster collaboration and partnerships: Digital transformation often requires collaboration and partnerships with other organizations and stakeholders. Leaders must be able to identify potential partners and collaborators, working together to create new opportunities for growth and innovation.

Focus on customer needs: Digital transformation must be driven by a focus on customer needs and preferences. Leaders must be able to understand their customers and their evolving needs, leveraging digital technologies to create personalized and engaging experiences.

Overall, by adopting these strategies, leaders can navigate the challenges and opportunities of digital transformation, creating value for customers and driving growth and success in the digital age.

Conclusion

In conclusion, digital transformation is fundamentally changing the way organizations operate, presenting significant challenges and opportunities for leaders. To succeed in the digital age, leaders must be able to navigate these challenges, adopting strategies that enable them to leverage emerging technologies, foster innovation, and create value for customers.

By developing a clear digital strategy, fostering a culture of innovation, investing in digital talent, embracing emerging technologies, fostering collaboration and partnerships, and focusing on customer needs, leaders can create a roadmap for success in the digital age.

Digital transformation is not a one-time event, but an ongoing process that requires leaders to be agile and adaptable in their approach. By adopting a growth mindset and a willingness to experiment and take risks, leaders can drive innovation and growth in their organization, creating value for their customers and staying ahead of the competition.

Ultimately, leadership in the digital age requires a combination of vision, strategic thinking, and an ability to execute on that vision. By embracing the challenges and opportunities of digital transformation, leaders can build organizations that are agile, innovative, and ready to succeed in the digital age.

2.

NAVIGATING THE TECHNOLOGICAL LANDSCAPE: KEY TRENDS AND TOOLS

In today's digital age, leaders must be familiar with the latest technological trends and tools to stay ahead of the curve. This chapter will explore some of the key trends and tools that are shaping the technological landscape and how leaders can navigate them.

Key Technological Trends

Artificial Intelligence (AI): AI is rapidly transforming the way organizations operate, enabling them to automate processes, improve decision-making, and enhance customer experiences. AI technologies such as machine learning, natural language processing, and computer vision are being used across a wide range of industries, from healthcare to finance to retail.

Cloud Computing: Cloud computing is becoming increasingly popular, allowing organizations to access and store data and applications over the internet. This technology enables organizations to scale their operations more efficiently and cost-effectively, as they do not need to invest in expensive hardware and infrastructure.

Internet of Things (IoT): The IoT is a network of physical devices, vehicles, home appliances, and other items embedded with sensors, software, and network connectivity, enabling them to collect and exchange data. This technology is being used to improve operational efficiency, reduce costs, and enhance customer experiences.

Blockchain: Blockchain is a decentralized, distributed ledger that records transactions securely and transparently. This technology is being used to create new business models and improve supply chain management, as well as enabling new forms of payment and financial transactions.

Key Technological Tools

Big Data Analytics: Big data analytics involves the collection and analysis of large, complex datasets to uncover insights and trends. This technology is being used to improve decision-making, optimize operations, and enhance customer experiences.

Customer Relationship Management (CRM) Software: CRM software is designed to help organizations manage their interactions with customers and improve customer relationships. This technology is being used to personalize customer experiences, improve sales and marketing, and increase customer loyalty.

Project Management Software: Project management software is used to plan, organize, and track tasks and resources for projects. This technology is being used to improve project management efficiency and collaboration, as well as to manage remote and distributed teams.

Cybersecurity Tools: Cybersecurity tools are designed to protect organizations from cyber threats and attacks, such as malware, phishing, and ransomware. This technology is being used to improve data security, reduce the risk of data breaches, and safeguard organizational assets.

Navigating the Technological Landscape

To navigate the technological landscape, leaders must be familiar with the latest trends and tools and how they can be applied to their organization's unique needs and challenges. Some key strategies for leaders to navigate the technological landscape include the following:

Identify key technological trends and tools that are relevant to your organization's needs and goals.

Develop a clear technology strategy that aligns with your organization's overall goals and objectives.

Invest in the right technological tools and resources, providing employees with the training and support they need to leverage these tools effectively.

Foster a culture of innovation and experimentation, encouraging employees to explore new technologies and find new ways to create value for customers.

Stay informed about the latest technological trends and tools, attending conferences, networking with peers, and staying up-to-date with industry publications and news.

Overall, by adopting these strategies, leaders can navigate the technological landscape, leveraging the latest trends and tools to create value for customers and drive growth and success in the digital age.

Key Technological Trends

In today's digital age, it is critical for leaders to stay abreast of the latest technological trends that are shaping the business landscape. These trends are rapidly transforming the way organizations operate, and failing to stay informed can put businesses at a competitive disadvantage. In this section, we will explore some of the key technological trends that are driving innovation and change.

Artificial Intelligence (AI)

Artificial intelligence (AI) has been one of the most transformative technological trends in recent years. AI refers to the ability of machines to learn from data and perform tasks that typically require human intelligence, such as recognizing speech, understanding natural language, and making decisions. AI is being used across a wide range of industries, from healthcare to finance to retail.

One of the most significant applications of AI is in automation. By automating routine tasks, organizations can reduce costs and free up employees to focus on more complex and strategic activities. AI is also being used to improve decision-making, providing insights and recommendations based on data analysis

Cloud Computing

Cloud computing has revolutionized the way organizations access and store data and applications. With cloud computing, data and applications are stored and accessed over the internet, rather than on local servers. This technology has enabled organizations to scale their operations more efficiently and cost-effectively, as they no longer need to invest in expensive hardware and infrastructure.

Cloud computing has also made it easier for organizations to collaborate and share information across teams and locations. This technology has enabled remote and distributed teams to work together seamlessly, improving productivity and efficiency.

Internet of Things (IoT)

The Internet of Things (IoT) is a network of physical devices, vehicles, home appliances, and other items embedded with sensors, software, and network connectivity, enabling them to collect and exchange data. IoT is being used to improve operational efficiency, reduce costs, and enhance customer experiences.

One of the most significant applications of IoT is in smart homes and buildings. By connecting appliances, lighting, and heating systems to the internet, organizations can automate routine tasks and reduce energy consumption. IoT is also being used in healthcare to monitor patients remotely, improving patient outcomes and reducing healthcare costs.

Blockchain

Blockchain is a decentralized, distributed ledger that records transactions securely and transparently. This technology has the potential to transform the way organizations conduct business, enabling new forms of payment and financial transactions, improving supply chain management, and creating new business models.
One of the most significant applications of blockchain is in cryptocurrencies such as Bitcoin. Blockchain enables secure, transparent, and decentralized transactions, reducing the need for intermediaries such as banks. Blockchain is also being used in supply chain management to improve transparency and reduce the risk of fraud and counterfeiting.

Augmented and Virtual Reality (AR/VR)

AR and VR technologies are enabling organizations to create immersive experiences for customers and employees. These technologies have the potential to revolutionize industries such as education, entertainment, and retail by enabling organizations to create realistic simulations and interactive experiences.

In conclusion, these key technological trends are rapidly transforming the business landscape, and leaders must be familiar with them to stay competitive. By embracing these trends, organizations can create new opportunities, improve efficiency, and enhance customer experiences.

Key Technological Tools

In addition to understanding technological trends, leaders must also be familiar with the tools and platforms that enable organizations to leverage these trends effectively. In this section, we will explore some of the key technological tools that are essential for organizations to navigate the digital landscape.

Customer Relationship Management (CRM) Software

CRM software is a platform that enables organizations to manage their interactions with customers and potential customers. This technology is essential for organizations to understand their customers' needs and preferences, as well as to deliver personalized experiences.

CRM software enables organizations to capture customer data, track customer interactions, and analyze customer behavior. This information can be used to develop targeted marketing campaigns, improve customer service, and drive customer loyalty.

Project Management Tools

Project management tools are essential for organizations to manage complex projects and initiatives. These tools enable teams to collaborate effectively, communicate with stakeholders, and track progress.

Project management tools typically include features such as task management, team communication, file sharing, and reporting. These tools can help teams stay organized, meet deadlines, and ensure that projects are completed successfully.

Social Media Platforms

Social media platforms are essential for organizations to connect with customers and build brand awareness. These platforms enable organizations to reach a wider audience, engage with customers, and respond to feedback and inquiries.

Social media platforms such as Facebook, Twitter, and LinkedIn provide organizations with a powerful tool for building relationships with customers and promoting their products and services. These platforms also enable organizations to gather valuable data on customer behavior and preferences.

Analytics Platforms

Analytics platforms are essential for organizations to measure their performance and identify areas for improvement. These platforms enable organizations to collect and analyze data on customer behavior, website traffic, and other key metrics.

Analytics platforms typically include features such as data visualization, data mining, and predictive analytics. These tools can help organizations to make data-driven decisions and optimize their operations for better performance.

In conclusion, these key technological tools are essential for organizations to leverage technological trends effectively. By investing in these tools and platforms, organizations can improve their operational efficiency, enhance customer experiences, and stay ahead of the competition.

Navigating the Technological Landscape

In order to navigate the technological landscape, leaders must stay informed about key trends and tools that are shaping the digital age. In this section, we will explore some of the key technological trends and tools that leaders must be aware of in order to drive innovation and remain competitive.

Cloud Computing

Cloud computing refers to the use of remote servers to store, manage, and process data. This technology has become increasingly popular in recent years due to its flexibility, scalability, and cost-effectiveness.

By leveraging cloud computing, organizations can reduce infrastructure costs and improve the efficiency of their

operations. Cloud computing also enables organizations to access data and applications from anywhere in the world, which can improve collaboration and productivity.
However, there are also concerns around data security and privacy, and leaders must be thoughtful about how they store and manage sensitive data in the cloud.

Big Data and Analytics

Big data and analytics refers to the use of advanced data analysis tools to identify patterns, insights, and trends in large data sets. This technology has become increasingly important in recent years as organizations generate more data than ever before.
By leveraging big data and analytics, organizations can gain valuable insights into customer behavior, market trends, and operational efficiency. This can enable organizations to make data-driven decisions and improve their overall performance.
However, there are also challenges around data quality, data governance, and data privacy, and leaders must be thoughtful about how they collect, store, and use data.

Cybersecurity

Cybersecurity refers to the protection of computer systems and networks from theft, damage, or unauthorized access. This is becoming increasingly important as organizations rely more heavily on technology to store and manage sensitive data.

By investing in cybersecurity, organizations can reduce the risk of data breaches, which can be costly in terms of both financial and reputational damage. Cybersecurity also enables organizations to protect their intellectual property and ensure compliance with regulatory requirements.

However, there are also challenges around the complexity of cybersecurity, and leaders must be thoughtful about how they allocate resources to ensure that their cybersecurity measures are effective.

In conclusion, navigating the technological landscape requires leaders to stay informed about key trends and tools that are shaping the digital age. Cloud computing, big data and analytics, and cybersecurity are just a few of the areas that leaders must be knowledgeable about in order to drive innovation and remain competitive in today's rapidly evolving business environment.

3.

THE ROLE OF DATA IN MODERN LEADERSHIP

In the digital age, data has become an essential component of business operations. Leaders who can effectively collect, analyze, and apply data have a significant advantage over their competitors. In this chapter, we will explore the role of data in modern leadership and how leaders can leverage data to drive innovation and success.

The Importance of Data-Driven Decision Making

Data-driven decision making involves using data to inform business decisions. Leaders who can effectively collect and analyze data can make more informed decisions that are based on facts and insights, rather than assumptions or guesswork. This approach can lead to better outcomes and increased success.

Collecting and Analyzing Data

To effectively use data to inform decision making, leaders must be able to collect and analyze data effectively. This requires investing in the right tools and resources, and hiring or training employees with the necessary skills to work with data.

Applying Data to Drive Innovation

Once data has been collected and analyzed, leaders must be able to apply the insights gained from the data to drive innovation and success. This may involve developing new products or services, improving existing offerings, or optimizing operations to improve efficiency and profitability.

Addressing Ethical Considerations

As with any use of technology, there are ethical considerations related to the use of data. Leaders must be aware of these considerations and ensure that data is collected and used in a responsible and ethical manner.

Conclusion

In conclusion, the role of data in modern leadership cannot be overstated. Leaders who can effectively collect, analyze, and apply data have a significant advantage in the digital age. By understanding the importance of data-driven decision making, investing in the right tools and resources, and addressing ethical considerations, leaders can use data to drive innovation and success in their organizations.

The Importance of Data-Driven Decision Making

Data-driven decision making has become increasingly important in the digital age. As more and more organizations rely on technology to collect and analyze data, leaders who can effectively use this data to inform decision making are better positioned to succeed.

One of the key benefits of data-driven decision making is that it helps leaders make more informed decisions. By collecting and analyzing data, leaders can gain insights into customer behavior, market trends, and internal operations that they may not have otherwise been aware of. This information can help leaders make more accurate predictions and informed decisions about everything from product development to marketing campaigns.

In addition to improving decision making, data-driven approaches can also help organizations optimize their operations. By analyzing data related to internal processes, leaders can identify areas for improvement and make changes that increase efficiency and profitability. For example, data can be used to identify bottlenecks in supply chains or to optimize production schedules.

Finally, data-driven decision making can help organizations stay ahead of their competitors. By leveraging data to inform their strategies, leaders can develop new products or services, enter new markets, or make other moves that can give them a competitive edge.

Overall, the importance of data-driven decision making cannot be overstated. By using data to inform decision making, leaders can make more informed decisions, optimize operations, and stay ahead of their competitors in the digital age.

Collecting and Analyzing Data

To effectively use data to inform decision making, leaders must have the right systems and processes in place for collecting and analyzing data. This requires a clear understanding of the types of data that are relevant to the organization's goals and objectives, as well as the tools and resources needed to effectively collect and analyze that data.

One of the first steps in collecting and analyzing data is identifying the key metrics that will be used to measure success. For example, a retail organization may track metrics related to sales, customer satisfaction, and inventory levels, while a healthcare organization may track metrics related to patient outcomes and satisfaction.

Once these metrics have been identified, leaders must determine the best methods for collecting data. This may involve collecting data manually, such as through surveys or interviews, or through automated systems, such as website analytics or sensors.

Once the data has been collected, it must be analyzed to identify patterns and insights that can inform decision making. This may involve using tools such as data visualization software or machine learning algorithms to identify trends and patterns in the data.

It's important to note that collecting and analyzing data is not a one-time process. Instead, it requires ongoing monitoring and analysis to ensure that the data being used to inform decision making is accurate and up-to-date. Additionally, as technology and business needs evolve, leaders must be prepared to adapt their data collection and analysis processes to ensure that they are effective in meeting the organization's goals and objectives.

Overall, collecting and analyzing data is a critical component of data-driven decision making. By understanding the types of data that are relevant to the organization's goals and objectives and using the right tools and processes to collect and analyze that data, leaders can make more informed decisions and drive success in the digital age.

Applying Data to Drive Innovation

Collecting and analyzing data is only the first step in using data to drive innovation in the digital age. The true value of data lies in its ability to inform decision-making and guide innovation efforts. Here are some key strategies for using data to drive innovation:

Identify customer pain points: By collecting and analyzing data on customer behavior, preferences, and feedback, leaders can gain insights into customer pain points and identify opportunities for innovation.

Develop targeted solutions: Armed with customer insights, leaders can develop targeted solutions that address specific pain points and deliver value to customers. This may involve leveraging emerging technologies, such as artificial intelligence and machine learning, to develop personalized solutions that meet the unique needs of each customer.

Test and iterate: Innovation is an iterative process, and leaders must be willing to test and refine their solutions based on feedback from customers and stakeholders. By using data to track the effectiveness of their solutions and iterate accordingly, leaders can continually improve their offerings and stay ahead of the competition.

Foster a data-driven culture: To truly leverage the power of data, leaders must foster a data-driven culture within their organization. This means empowering employees to collect and analyze data, encouraging them to make decisions based on data insights, and providing them with the tools and resources they need to effectively use data to drive innovation.

By applying data to drive innovation, leaders can create more effective solutions, meet the evolving needs of customers, and stay ahead of the competition in the digital age. However, it is important to remember that data alone is not enough – leaders must also possess the skills and mindset to effectively use data to inform decision-making and drive innovation.

Addressing Ethical Considerations

As leaders increasingly rely on data to drive decision making, it is essential to address the ethical considerations surrounding data collection, storage, and usage. Organizations must prioritize data privacy, security, and transparency to build trust with customers and stakeholders.

One key ethical consideration is data privacy. Leaders must ensure that customer data is collected and stored in a secure manner and only used for its intended purposes. Any data breaches must be promptly reported and addressed to maintain trust with customers.

Another consideration is the potential for bias in data analysis. Leaders must ensure that they are using unbiased data sources and analysis methods to avoid making decisions that could negatively impact certain groups or individuals.

Finally, transparency is crucial in ensuring ethical data practices. Leaders must communicate clearly about their data collection and usage policies and be open to feedback and questions from customers and stakeholders.

Overall, by addressing these ethical considerations and prioritizing data privacy, security, and transparency, leaders can ensure that data is used in a responsible and ethical manner to drive innovation and success in the digital age.

Conclusion

In conclusion, data-driven decision making is an essential component of modern leadership. By collecting and analyzing data, leaders can make informed decisions that drive innovation and success while prioritizing ethical considerations such as data privacy, security, and transparency.

Leaders must also be willing to embrace new technologies and tools that can help them collect, analyze, and apply data in meaningful ways. By doing so, they can create a culture of innovation and experimentation that drives growth and creates value for customers, employees, and stakeholders.

In today's rapidly changing digital landscape, leaders who prioritize data-driven decision making will be better equipped to navigate change and drive innovation. By adopting the strategies and tools discussed in this chapter, leaders can leverage data to make informed decisions and position their organizations for success in the digital age.

4.

CREATING A CULTURE OF INNOVATION: PRINCIPLES AND PRACTICES

Innovation is a critical driver of success in the digital age, and leaders must create a culture that fosters creativity, experimentation, and continuous improvement. This chapter will explore the principles and practices of creating a culture of innovation within an organization.

Defining a Culture of Innovation
What is a culture of innovation?
Why is a culture of innovation important?
How does a culture of innovation differ from a traditional organizational culture?

Principles of Creating a Culture of Innovation
Encouraging creativity and experimentation
Embracing failure and learning from mistakes
Supporting risk-taking and calculated risk
Nurturing diverse perspectives and inclusivity
Building a sense of purpose and shared vision

Practices for Creating a Culture of Innovation

Providing time and resources for innovation
Recognizing and rewarding innovative ideas and outcomes
Encouraging collaboration and cross-functional teams
Building a culture of continuous learning and development
Empowering employees to take ownership of innovation

Measuring the Impact of a Culture of Innovation
Defining success metrics for innovation
Tracking progress and outcomes
Incorporating feedback and making adjustments

Conclusion
Creating a culture of innovation is a key element in achieving success in the digital age. By defining the principles and practices of innovation and creating a supportive environment, leaders can drive innovation, improve organizational performance, and create value for customers and stakeholders. This chapter will provide practical strategies for leaders to create a culture of innovation within their organizations.

Defining a Culture of Innovation

Innovation is critical for organizations seeking to thrive in the digital age. To foster innovation, leaders must cultivate a culture that encourages creativity, experimentation, and risk-taking. This culture of innovation is characterized by several key principles and practices that are essential to driving growth and success in the digital age.

At its core, a culture of innovation is a mindset that encourages individuals and teams to think outside the box, challenge the status quo, and pursue new ideas and opportunities. This mindset is supported by several key principles, including a commitment to continuous improvement, a willingness to take calculated risks, and an emphasis on collaboration and cross-functional teams. To create a culture of innovation, leaders must also adopt several key practices, including the following:

Encouraging experimentation and prototyping
Embracing failure as a learning opportunity
Providing resources and support for innovation initiatives
Recognizing and rewarding innovative ideas and contributions
Creating an environment of trust and psychological safety that encourages open communication and feedback

By adopting these principles and practices, leaders can create a culture of innovation that supports continuous growth and success in the digital age.

Principles of Creating a Culture of Innovation

To create a culture of innovation within an organization, leaders need to establish clear principles that guide behavior and decision-making at every level of the organization. Some key principles of creating a culture of innovation include:

Foster a Growth Mindset: A growth mindset is an attitude that embraces learning, improvement, and experimentation. Leaders must encourage employees to adopt a growth mindset and be willing to take risks and try new things.

Encourage Collaboration: Collaboration is essential for innovation. Leaders must encourage employees to work together, share ideas, and collaborate on projects.

Embrace Diversity: Diversity in perspectives, experiences, and backgrounds is essential for innovation. Leaders must create a culture that values and encourages diversity and inclusion.

Empower Employees: Innovation requires autonomy and empowerment. Leaders must provide employees with the resources, support, and freedom they need to experiment and innovate.

Emphasize Customer Focus: Innovation is about creating value for customers. Leaders must ensure that customer needs and feedback are integrated into every aspect of the innovation process.

Reward and Recognize Innovation: Innovation should be celebrated and rewarded within the organization. Leaders must establish clear recognition and reward systems that encourage and incentivize innovation.

By establishing these principles and embedding them into the organizational culture, leaders can create a culture of innovation that drives growth, creativity, and success.

Practices for Creating a Culture of Innovation

Creating a culture of innovation requires more than just adopting the right principles - it requires taking concrete actions and implementing practices that foster creativity, experimentation, and risk-taking. Here are some key practices that can help leaders create a culture of innovation within their organizations:

Encourage experimentation: Encourage employees to experiment with new ideas and approaches, and create a safe environment where they feel comfortable taking risks and trying new things.

Foster collaboration: Foster a collaborative environment where employees are encouraged to work together, share ideas, and build on each other's strengths.

Provide resources: Provide employees with the resources they need to explore new ideas and develop innovative solutions, whether it's access to cutting-edge technology, funding for research and development, or time to experiment.

Recognize and reward innovation: Recognize and reward employees who demonstrate innovative thinking and contribute to the organization's culture of innovation. This can take the form of bonuses, promotions, or other incentives that encourage creativity and risk-taking.

Lead by example: Leaders must lead by example and demonstrate a commitment to innovation in their own actions and decisions. This can involve setting aside time for creative thinking, actively seeking out new ideas and perspectives, and taking calculated risks to drive growth and success.

By implementing these practices and taking a proactive approach to building a culture of innovation, leaders can foster a dynamic and creative environment that drives growth, success, and long-term sustainability.

Measuring the Impact of a Culture of Innovation

Creating a culture of innovation is a key goal for many organizations, but how can leaders measure the impact of their efforts? There are several metrics that can be used to measure the success of a culture of innovation:

Employee Engagement: When employees are engaged, they are more likely to come up with new ideas and take risks. Measuring employee engagement through surveys and feedback can give leaders a sense of how engaged their workforce is.

Idea Generation: The number and quality of ideas generated is another metric that can be used to measure the success of a culture of innovation. This can be tracked through idea management software, brainstorming sessions, and other idea-generation processes.

Time to Market: A culture of innovation should lead to faster development and delivery of new products and services. Measuring the time it takes to bring new products to market can indicate whether the culture of innovation is having a positive impact.

Revenue Growth: Ultimately, the success of a culture of innovation should be reflected in the organization's financial performance. Measuring revenue growth, particularly from new products or services, can indicate whether the culture of innovation is creating value for customers.

By tracking these metrics and using them to adjust and refine their innovation strategies, leaders can ensure that their efforts to create a culture of innovation are having a positive impact on the organization.

Conclusion

In conclusion, creating a culture of innovation is essential for organizations that want to thrive in the digital age. By defining a culture of innovation and applying the principles and practices outlined in this chapter, leaders can foster an environment where creativity, experimentation, and risk-taking are encouraged and celebrated. This not only leads to new products and services but also enhances the organization's ability to adapt to change and drive continuous improvement. By measuring the impact of a culture of innovation, leaders can also ensure that their efforts are paying off and identify areas for improvement. In the next chapter, we will explore the importance of building diverse and inclusive teams in driving innovation and success.

5.

EMPOWERING AND ENCOURAGING CREATIVITY: STRATEGIES FOR SUCCESS

In today's fast-paced digital world, creativity is more important than ever before. Leaders must empower and encourage creativity within their organizations to stay ahead of the competition and drive innovation. This chapter will explore the following strategies for success in fostering creativity:

Creating a Safe Space for Creativity
Establishing an environment of psychological safety where employees feel comfortable expressing their ideas
Encouraging diverse perspectives and open communication

Creating a culture of experimentation and learning from failure

Providing Resources and Support for Creative Work
Providing access to the necessary tools and technologies
Offering training and development opportunities
Supporting cross-functional collaboration and teamwork

Encouraging Autonomy and Empowering Employees
Providing autonomy and flexibility to employees to pursue creative solutions
Empowering employees to take ownership of their work and ideas
Encouraging risk-taking and exploration

Recognizing and Celebrating Creativity
Creating a system of rewards and recognition for creative work
Celebrating successes and sharing lessons learned
Encouraging a culture of gratitude and appreciation

Measuring the Impact of Creativity
Defining metrics to measure the impact of creativity on business outcomes
Using data to evaluate the success of creativity initiatives
Continuously iterating and improving creative processes and practices based on feedback and results

Conclusion

By implementing these strategies, leaders can create a culture of innovation and creativity within their organizations, driving growth and success in the digital age. Empowering and encouraging creativity can be a key differentiator in a competitive market and can enable organizations to stay ahead of the curve in a rapidly changing business environment.

Creating a Safe Space for Creativity

Creativity is essential for driving innovation, but it can be challenging to cultivate in the workplace. Leaders must create a safe space where employees feel comfortable sharing their ideas and taking risks. Here are some strategies for creating a safe space for creativity:

Foster a positive and inclusive workplace culture: Leaders should cultivate a workplace culture that encourages diversity, inclusivity, and collaboration. When employees feel included, they are more likely to feel comfortable sharing their ideas.

Encourage risk-taking: Leaders should create an environment where it is safe to take risks and make mistakes. Employees should feel empowered to try new things without fear of repercussions.

Provide opportunities for professional development: Leaders should provide employees with training and development opportunities to help them improve their skills and stay up-to-date with industry trends. This will help them feel more confident in their abilities and more willing to take risks.

Create a feedback loop: Leaders should create a feedback loop where employees can share their ideas and receive constructive feedback. This will help employees feel valued and supported in their creative endeavors.

Celebrate success: Leaders should celebrate successes, no matter how small they may be. This will encourage employees to continue taking risks and sharing their ideas.

By creating a safe space for creativity, leaders can empower their employees to take risks, share their ideas, and drive innovation in the organization.

Providing Resources and Support for Creative Work

To empower and encourage creativity, leaders must provide their employees with the resources and support they need to bring their ideas to life. Here are some strategies for providing resources and support for creative work:

Allocating Time and Resources: One of the most important resources that leaders can provide is time. Creativity cannot be rushed, and employees need time to experiment and explore ideas. Leaders should allocate dedicated time for creative work, such as "innovation hours" or "hackathons," where employees can work on passion projects and experiment with new ideas. Additionally, leaders should allocate financial resources to support creative work, such as funding for research and development, prototyping, and testing.

Providing Access to Tools and Technology: Creativity often requires specialized tools and technology. Leaders should provide their employees with access to the tools and technology they need to bring their ideas to life. This could include providing access to specialized software, equipment, or materials, or providing training and support for new tools and technologies.

Encouraging Collaboration and Diversity of Thought: Creativity thrives in environments that encourage collaboration and diversity of thought. Leaders should create opportunities for cross-functional teams to work together and share ideas. Additionally, leaders should promote diversity and inclusivity in their hiring practices, creating teams with diverse backgrounds and perspectives.

Celebrating Successes and Learning from Failures: Celebrating successes and learning from failures is critical to fostering a culture of creativity. Leaders should recognize and celebrate the successes of their employees, providing positive feedback and recognition for their creative work. Additionally, leaders should embrace failure as a learning opportunity, encouraging employees to take risks and learn from their mistakes.

By providing resources and support for creative work, leaders can empower their employees to think outside the box and bring innovative ideas to life. This can drive growth and success in the digital age and help organizations stay competitive in a rapidly changing market.

Encouraging Autonomy and Empowering Employees

One of the most important aspects of fostering a culture of creativity and innovation is empowering employees with the autonomy to explore and experiment with new ideas. When employees are given the freedom to take risks and try new things, they are more likely to develop novel solutions and generate innovative ideas.

Leaders can empower employees by providing them with the resources and support they need to explore new ideas, including time, funding, and access to tools and technologies. Additionally, leaders can encourage autonomy by providing employees with clear goals and objectives, but giving them the flexibility to determine how they will achieve these goals.

To further encourage autonomy and empowerment, leaders can also provide opportunities for employees to take ownership of projects and initiatives, allowing them to work on projects that align with their interests and passions.

However, it's important to note that encouraging autonomy does not mean abandoning leadership altogether. Leaders must still provide guidance and direction, ensuring that employees are aligned with the organization's goals and values. By balancing autonomy and guidance, leaders can empower employees to explore new ideas and take ownership of their work while still achieving the organization's broader objectives.

Ultimately, empowering employees with autonomy is a key strategy for fostering creativity and innovation, allowing employees to take risks, explore new ideas, and generate novel solutions to complex problems.

Recognizing and Celebrating Creativity

Recognizing and celebrating creativity is an essential component of creating a culture of innovation. When employees feel that their ideas and contributions are valued and appreciated, they are more likely to be motivated to continue creating and innovating. Here are some strategies for recognizing and celebrating creativity in the workplace:

Celebrate successes: When a team or individual achieves a breakthrough, celebrate their success publicly. This can be as simple as sending an email to the team or publicly acknowledging their success in a meeting.

Provide incentives: Consider providing incentives for employees who contribute innovative ideas or who go above and beyond in their creative work. This could be in the form of bonuses, promotions, or other rewards.

Encourage peer recognition: Encourage employees to recognize and celebrate their colleagues' creativity. This could be through a peer recognition program or by simply giving a shout-out in a team meeting.

Showcase creativity: Display examples of creative work in prominent areas of the workplace, such as the lobby or break room. This can help inspire others and create a sense of pride and ownership in the organization's creative work.

Provide opportunities for professional development: Encourage employees to continue learning and growing in their creative skills by providing opportunities for professional development, such as workshops, training sessions, or conferences.

By recognizing and celebrating creativity, leaders can foster a culture of innovation where employees feel empowered to take risks and contribute their ideas, ultimately driving growth and success for the organization.

Measuring the Impact of Creativity

While creativity is often seen as difficult to measure, it is important for leaders to understand the impact that creativity is having on their organization. By measuring the impact of creativity, leaders can better understand how it is driving innovation, improving performance, and enhancing customer satisfaction. Here are some key metrics that leaders can use to measure the impact of creativity:

Innovation metrics: This includes metrics such as the number of new products, services, or processes that have been introduced as a result of creative efforts. Other innovation metrics might include the number of patents filed or the number of industry awards won.

Performance metrics: These metrics might include measures of productivity, efficiency, or quality. Leaders can look for improvements in these metrics that might be attributed to creative efforts. For example, if a creative approach to product design has resulted in faster production times or higher quality products, this could be reflected in performance metrics.

Customer satisfaction metrics: Leaders can also look at metrics related to customer satisfaction, such as customer retention rates, NPS scores, or customer reviews. By looking at these metrics before and after creative efforts have been implemented, leaders can get a sense of whether creativity is having a positive impact on customer satisfaction.

Employee engagement metrics: Finally, leaders can look at employee engagement metrics to understand the impact of creativity on the workforce. For example, if employees are more engaged in their work or more likely to stay with the organization as a result of creative initiatives, this could be reflected in metrics such as employee turnover rates or employee satisfaction scores.

Overall, by measuring the impact of creativity, leaders can gain a better understanding of how it is driving innovation and enhancing performance in their organization. This can help leaders to better allocate resources and support creative initiatives that are having the greatest impact.

Conclusion

In conclusion, creativity is a critical element for driving innovation and success in the digital age. By creating a safe space for creativity, providing resources and support for creative work, encouraging autonomy and empowerment, and recognizing and celebrating creativity, leaders can cultivate an environment that empowers employees to think outside the box, take risks, and generate new ideas. Measuring the impact of creativity through key performance indicators such as revenue growth, customer satisfaction, and employee engagement can also help leaders to quantify the value of creativity and ensure that it remains a priority for the organization. By adopting these strategies and fostering a culture of creativity, leaders can unlock the full potential of their employees, drive innovation, and position their organizations for long-term success in an increasingly competitive and rapidly evolving digital landscape.

6.

THE IMPORTANCE OF FAILURE: LEARNING FROM SETBACKS AND MISTAKES

While success is often the goal, failure is an inevitable part of any journey. In the realm of business and leadership, failure can be particularly challenging, as it can impact not only individuals but entire teams or organizations. However, it's important to recognize that failure can also be an opportunity for growth and learning. This chapter will explore the importance of failure and how leaders can create a culture that encourages experimentation and risk-taking while also learning from setbacks and mistakes.

Redefining Failure

The negative connotations associated with failure and the fear of failure

The benefits of redefining failure as a learning opportunity and the power of reframing one's mindset

Creating a Safe Space for Failure

How leaders can create a culture that supports experimentation and risk-taking
Encouraging transparency and communication to build trust and reduce fear of failure
Providing resources and support for employees to take calculated risks and learn from mistakes

Learning from Failure
Strategies for reflecting on and analyzing failures to extract lessons learned
Encouraging open and honest communication to share learnings across the organization
Using failure as an opportunity for growth and innovation

Moving Forward
The importance of using failure as a stepping stone to success
Implementing changes and improvements based on lessons learned from failures
Encouraging a growth mindset and continuous learning and development

Conclusion
Failure can be a difficult and even painful experience, but it's important for leaders to recognize its value as a learning opportunity. By redefining failure, creating a safe space for experimentation, and learning from setbacks and mistakes, leaders can help their teams and organizations grow and thrive. Ultimately, embracing failure can lead to greater innovation, stronger teams, and more successful outcomes.

Redefining Failure

Traditionally, failure has been seen as something to be avoided at all costs, with little to no room for mistakes or missteps. However, in the modern business landscape, failure is being redefined as an essential part of the innovation process.

Rather than being a cause for shame or punishment, failure is now seen as an opportunity for learning and growth. Many successful companies and leaders have embraced a "fail fast, fail forward" mentality, where they encourage experimentation and risk-taking in order to quickly identify what works and what doesn't.

By redefining failure in this way, leaders can create a more open and collaborative work environment, where employees feel empowered to take risks and try new things without fear of retribution. This can lead to increased innovation, creativity, and ultimately, success.

Creating a Safe Space for Failure

Creating a safe space for failure is crucial for organizations to foster innovation and growth. It involves creating a culture where employees are encouraged to take risks, experiment, and learn from their mistakes without fear of punishment or negative consequences. Here are some strategies for leaders to create a safe space for failure:

Emphasize learning and growth: Leaders should emphasize the importance of learning and growth over avoiding mistakes. This means reframing failures as opportunities for learning and improvement, rather than something to be avoided at all costs.

Encourage open communication: Leaders should encourage open and honest communication, where employees feel comfortable sharing their failures and mistakes without fear of judgment or retribution. This creates a culture of transparency and trust, where everyone is working together to improve and innovate.

Provide support and resources: Leaders should provide the necessary resources and support for employees to experiment and take risks. This includes providing training, mentorship, and access to tools and technology.

Lead by example: Leaders should lead by example and demonstrate that failure is not something to be ashamed of or punished. They should be open about their own failures and share how they learned and grew from them.

By creating a safe space for failure, leaders can encourage creativity and innovation while also empowering their employees to take risks and learn from their mistakes. This leads to a more resilient and adaptive organization that is better equipped to navigate the challenges of the modern business landscape.

Learning from Failure

While failure may be uncomfortable or even painful, it can also be an opportunity for growth and learning. Leaders can help their teams learn from failure by following these practices:

Encourage reflection and analysis: When a failure occurs, it's important to take time to reflect on what happened and why. Encourage your team to analyze the situation, identify what went wrong, and consider what could have been done differently.
Promote experimentation: Encourage your team to try new things and take risks. Foster a culture of experimentation where it's safe to fail and where failure is seen as a valuable learning opportunity.
Emphasize learning over blame: When a failure occurs, avoid the temptation to blame individuals or teams. Instead, focus on what can be learned from the experience and how the organization can improve.
Provide support and resources: Make sure your team has the resources and support they need to learn from failure. This might include training, coaching, or additional resources to help them improve.
Celebrate successes and failures: Celebrate both successes and failures to create a culture that values growth and learning. When a team or individual learns from failure and makes positive changes, recognize and celebrate their efforts.

By adopting these practices, leaders can create a culture where failure is seen as an opportunity for growth and learning, rather than a negative outcome to be avoided at all costs. This mindset can help teams become more resilient and adaptable, and better able to navigate challenges and uncertainty.

Moving Forward

While it is important to learn from failure, it is equally important to move forward and take action based on the lessons learned. This can involve several key steps:

Reframe failure as an opportunity: Rather than seeing failure as a negative experience, leaders should strive to reframe it as an opportunity for growth and improvement. By adopting this mindset, leaders can help their teams view failure in a more positive light and encourage them to take risks and experiment.

Identify and address root causes: When a failure occurs, it is important to identify and address the underlying causes. This involves a thorough analysis of the situation, including an examination of the processes, systems, and behaviors that contributed to the failure.

Implement changes and improvements: Based on the lessons learned, leaders should take action to implement changes and improvements. This may involve changes to processes or systems, adjustments to team dynamics, or improvements to training and support.

Communicate and share learnings: Finally, it is important to communicate the learnings from failure and share them with the wider organization. This can help to create a culture of continuous improvement and encourage others to take risks and learn from failure.

By taking these steps, leaders can help their teams learn from failure and use it as a stepping stone to future success.

Conclusion

In conclusion, failure is an inevitable part of the journey towards success, and it is crucial for leaders to understand its importance. By redefining failure, creating a safe space for it, and learning from it, leaders can turn setbacks and mistakes into valuable opportunities for growth and innovation. Additionally, moving forward from failure requires a willingness to take risks, a growth mindset, and a focus on continuous learning and improvement. Leaders who can embrace failure as an opportunity for learning and growth can create a culture of resilience, creativity, and innovation in their organization.

7.

LEADING CHANGE: THE IMPORTANCE OF VISION AND COMMUNICATION

Change is inevitable in any organization, and it is the responsibility of leaders to navigate their teams through change successfully. In today's fast-paced business world, change is happening more rapidly than ever, making it essential for leaders to have a clear vision and effective communication skills. This chapter will explore the importance of vision and communication in leading change, and provide strategies for successfully navigating change within an organization.

The Role of Vision in Leading Change

A clear and compelling vision is essential for guiding an organization through change. A vision is a picture of the future that leaders want to create, and it serves as a beacon that guides decision-making and actions. A strong vision provides a sense of direction and purpose, inspiring and motivating employees to work towards a common goal. Leaders who can communicate their vision effectively are more likely to gain buy-in from their team members and achieve successful change.

The Importance of Communication in Leading Change

Effective communication is key to successfully leading change. Leaders must be able to communicate their vision and goals clearly and concisely to their team members, and ensure that everyone understands what is expected of them. Communication should be frequent and transparent, allowing team members to ask questions and provide feedback. Leaders must also be able to adapt their communication style to meet the needs of different team members and stakeholders, tailoring their message to be relevant and engaging.

Strategies for Leading Change

To successfully lead change, leaders must have a solid plan in place, with clear goals and objectives. They must also be able to identify potential obstacles and challenges, and have contingency plans in place to address them. Leaders must build trust and foster open communication with their team members, ensuring that everyone is aligned and working towards the same goal. They must also be willing to listen to feedback and adjust their approach as needed.

The Role of Emotional Intelligence in Leading Change

Emotional intelligence is the ability to recognize and manage one's own emotions, as well as those of others. Leaders who possess emotional intelligence are better equipped to navigate change successfully, as they are more attuned to the needs and concerns of their team members. They are able to communicate effectively, build trust, and inspire and motivate others to achieve their goals.

Conclusion

Leading change is a complex and challenging task, but with a clear vision and effective communication skills, leaders can successfully navigate their organizations through change. By focusing on building trust, fostering open communication, and cultivating emotional intelligence, leaders can inspire and motivate their team members to work towards a common goal and achieve successful change.

The Role of Vision in Leading Change

In order to effectively lead change, a leader must have a clear and compelling vision for the future. A vision is a mental image of what the future could look like, and it serves as a guide for action and decision-making.

A vision should be ambitious, yet realistic, and it should align with the organization's overall mission and values. It should also be communicated clearly and consistently to all stakeholders, including employees, customers, and investors.

A strong vision can inspire and motivate employees, create a sense of purpose and direction, and guide decision-making at all levels of the organization. It can also serve as a rallying point for stakeholders and help build support for change initiatives.

However, developing and communicating a clear and compelling vision is not enough on its own. Leaders must also be able to effectively communicate the vision and the reasons for change to all stakeholders, including those who may be resistant to change. This requires strong communication skills and the ability to listen to and address concerns and feedback from all stakeholders.

In summary, a clear and compelling vision is essential for leading change. It provides a sense of purpose and direction, guides decision-making, and inspires and motivates employees and stakeholders. Effective communication of the vision is also critical to building support and addressing resistance to change.

The Importance of Communication in Leading Change

In order for change to be successful, effective communication is essential. Leaders must be able to clearly articulate their vision for change, why it is necessary, and how it will benefit the organization and its stakeholders. This requires not only effective verbal communication but also the ability to use various communication channels such as email, social media, and town hall meetings to reach a wide audience.

There are several key principles of effective communication in the context of leading change:

Transparency: Leaders must be open and honest with their stakeholders about the reasons for change, what the change will entail, and what the expected outcomes are. This builds trust and credibility with stakeholders, which is critical for successful change.

Consistency: Communication about change must be consistent across all channels and all levels of the organization. This helps to ensure that all stakeholders have the same understanding of what is happening and why.

Listening: Effective communication is a two-way process. Leaders must listen to feedback and concerns from stakeholders and incorporate them into their plans for change where appropriate.

Clarity: Communication about change must be clear and concise, using language that is easy to understand and avoiding technical jargon or buzzwords that can confuse stakeholders.

Timing: Communication about change must be timely, with updates provided at regular intervals and in response to significant events or milestones in the change process.

Empathy: Leaders must be able to understand and empathize with the concerns and emotions of stakeholders who may be affected by the change. This requires active listening and an ability to put oneself in the shoes of others.

In addition to these principles, leaders must also consider the different communication preferences and needs of different stakeholders. For example, some employees may prefer face-to-face communication, while others may prefer email or social media updates. It is important to tailor communication to the needs and preferences of different groups to ensure that everyone is informed and engaged in the change process.

Overall, effective communication is a critical component of leading change. By using principles of transparency, consistency, listening, clarity, timing, and empathy, leaders can build trust and credibility with stakeholders and create a shared understanding of the vision for change.

Strategies for Leading Change

Leading change can be a complex and challenging process, but there are several strategies that can help leaders effectively guide their organizations through periods of transition. Here are some key strategies for leading change:

Develop a clear vision: To effectively lead change, leaders must have a clear vision of where they want to take their organization. This vision should be articulated in a way that inspires and motivates employees, and should be grounded in a deep understanding of the organization's strengths, weaknesses, and opportunities.

Communicate the vision: Once the vision has been developed, it is essential that leaders communicate it clearly and effectively to all stakeholders. This involves not only articulating the vision in a way that is easy to understand, but also engaging in ongoing communication with employees to ensure that they understand and support the vision.

Build a coalition of support: Leading change is rarely a solo effort. To be successful, leaders must build a coalition of support among key stakeholders, including employees, customers, and partners. This coalition can help drive the change initiative forward and provide critical support when obstacles arise.

Create a sense of urgency: To successfully lead change, leaders must create a sense of urgency around the need for change. This involves articulating the risks and opportunities associated with the change initiative, and engaging employees in a discussion about why change is necessary.

Empower employees: Change initiatives are more likely to be successful when employees feel empowered to take ownership of the process. Leaders should provide employees with the training, resources, and support they need to participate in the change initiative, and should encourage them to take an active role in driving the process forward.

Celebrate successes: Change initiatives can be challenging and often involve setbacks and obstacles. To keep employees motivated and engaged, it is important to celebrate successes along the way, no matter how small they may be.

By adopting these strategies, leaders can effectively lead change and create a culture of innovation and growth within their organizations.

The Role of Emotional Intelligence in Leading Change

Emotional intelligence, or EQ, plays a critical role in leading change. EQ is the ability to understand and manage emotions, both in oneself and others. When leading change, it is essential to recognize the emotions of those affected by the change and to manage those emotions effectively.

One of the key elements of EQ is empathy, which involves understanding and sharing the feelings of others. Leaders who are empathetic can better understand the impact that change has on their employees, which enables them to provide the support and guidance needed during the transition.

Another important element of EQ is self-awareness, which involves understanding one's own emotions and how they impact others. Leaders who are self-aware are better equipped to manage their own emotions and reactions, which in turn helps them to respond effectively to the emotions of others during times of change.

In addition to empathy and self-awareness, EQ also includes skills such as social awareness and relationship management. Leaders who possess these skills are able to build trust and rapport with their employees, which is essential when leading change.

When it comes to leading change, it is important to communicate the vision for the change in a way that resonates with employees emotionally. This requires leaders to be able to communicate with clarity, transparency, and authenticity. By communicating with empathy and understanding, leaders can help their employees to feel heard, valued, and supported during the change process.

Overall, EQ plays a critical role in leading change, as it enables leaders to connect with their employees on an emotional level and manage the emotions that arise during times of transition. By developing EQ skills, leaders can lead change effectively and help their employees navigate the change process with greater ease and resilience.

Conclusion

In today's rapidly changing business environment, effective leadership is crucial to driving change and innovation. As highlighted in this chapter, having a clear vision and effective communication are key components of successful change leadership. By articulating a compelling vision that inspires and motivates employees, leaders can create a shared sense of purpose and direction, fostering a culture of innovation and growth. Additionally, effective communication is critical to ensuring that all stakeholders are aligned and informed, reducing resistance to change and increasing engagement and buy-in.

Moreover, the strategies discussed in this chapter, such as creating a sense of urgency, involving stakeholders in the change process, and leveraging emotional intelligence, can help leaders navigate the complex challenges of change management. By adopting these strategies, leaders can build trust and credibility, inspire confidence and commitment, and drive meaningful change that delivers value to all stakeholders.

In conclusion, leading change is an essential skill for modern leaders, and vision and communication are the cornerstones of successful change leadership. By embracing these principles and strategies, leaders can create a culture of innovation, drive growth and success, and build a resilient and agile organization that can adapt and thrive in today's dynamic business landscape.

8.

OVERCOMING RESISTANCE TO CHANGE: STRATEGIES AND TECHNIQUES

Change is an inevitable part of any organization's journey towards growth and success. However, it is often met with resistance from employees who are comfortable with the status quo or fear the unknown. Therefore, it is crucial for leaders to understand how to overcome resistance to change effectively. This chapter will discuss various strategies and techniques that can help leaders to overcome resistance to change.

Understanding Resistance to Change
Definition of resistance to change
Reasons for resistance to change
Types of resistance to change
Impact of resistance to change on the organization

Strategies to Overcome Resistance to Change
Effective communication

Creating a sense of urgency
Involving employees in the change process
Building a coalition of support
Offering incentives and rewards
Training and development
Addressing concerns and fears
Making change manageable

Techniques for Overcoming Resistance to Change
Education and information sharing
Participation and involvement
Facilitation and support
Negotiation and compromise
Coercion and force

Addressing Resistance to Change in Different Contexts
Addressing resistance to change in a global context
Addressing resistance to change in a diverse workplace
Addressing resistance to change in a crisis situation
Addressing resistance to change in a digital transformation

Conclusion
Overcoming resistance to change is a challenging but necessary task for leaders who want to lead their organizations towards growth and success. By understanding the reasons for resistance to change, implementing effective strategies and techniques, and addressing resistance in different contexts, leaders can

create a culture of openness to change, leading to increased innovation, productivity, and success.

Understanding Resistance to Change

Change is often necessary for an organization to grow and succeed, but it can also be met with resistance from employees who are comfortable with the status quo or fear the unknown. As a leader, it is essential to understand the various reasons for resistance to change and to develop strategies to overcome them.

One reason for resistance to change is the fear of the unknown. Employees may feel uncertain about how the change will impact their job responsibilities, their relationship with colleagues, or the overall direction of the organization. Additionally, they may feel threatened by the change and fear that it could lead to job loss or a decline in their status within the organization.

Another reason for resistance to change is a lack of trust in leadership or the change process. If employees feel that their input is not valued or that the change is being imposed without their consultation, they may be less likely to embrace it. Additionally, if past changes have not been successful, employees may be skeptical about the potential benefits of the current change.

Lastly, resistance to change can also stem from a lack of understanding or training. Employees may not have the necessary skills or knowledge to adapt to the change, which can lead to frustration and resistance.

As a leader, it is important to acknowledge and address these reasons for resistance to change. By doing so, you can develop strategies and techniques that can help overcome resistance and successfully implement the desired changes.

1.1 Definition of resistance to change

Resistance to change refers to the natural and common human tendency to resist or avoid change, particularly when it impacts our work or personal lives. It is often rooted in fear, uncertainty, and a desire to maintain the status quo. Resistance to change can manifest in a variety of ways, such as active resistance, passive resistance, skepticism, and denial, and can have significant implications for organizational success and individual well-being. As such, it is important for leaders to understand resistance to change and develop strategies for overcoming it.

1.2 Reasons for resistance to change

Resistance to change is a common phenomenon in organizations, and it can take many forms, including passive resistance, active resistance, and even sabotage. Resistance to change can be caused by a wide range of factors, including:

Fear of the unknown: People are often uncomfortable with uncertainty and the unknown, which can cause them to resist change that disrupts their familiar routines.
Loss of control: Change can also threaten people's sense of control and autonomy, which can be a significant source of anxiety and resistance.

Fear of failure: People may resist change because they fear that it will lead to failure or negative consequences, either for themselves or for the organization as a whole.

Lack of trust: If employees do not trust their leaders or the change process, they may be more likely to resist change.

Organizational politics: Resistance to change can also be driven by power struggles, rivalries, and other political dynamics within the organization.

Cultural differences: Differences in culture, values, and norms can also lead to resistance to change, particularly if the change is seen as threatening or incompatible with these values.

Inadequate communication: When leaders fail to communicate clearly about the reasons for change and how it will impact employees, this can lead to confusion, anxiety, and resistance.

Overall, it is essential for leaders to understand the reasons for resistance to change so that they can anticipate and address these challenges effectively. By taking proactive steps to address resistance, leaders can help ensure that change initiatives are successful and that the organization is able to adapt and thrive in a rapidly changing environment.

1.3 Types of resistance to change

Resistance to change is a common phenomenon in organizations, and it can take many forms. Leaders must be able to recognize and understand the different types of resistance to change so they can develop effective strategies to overcome them. Here are some common types of resistance to change:

Emotional Resistance: Emotional resistance to change is often driven by fear, anxiety, or a sense of loss. Employees may worry about losing their jobs, their status, or their sense of belonging. They may also fear the unknown or feel overwhelmed by the amount of change they are being asked to undertake.

Cognitive Resistance: Cognitive resistance is often driven by a lack of understanding or a belief that the change is unnecessary or even harmful. Employees may resist change because they don't understand the rationale behind it or because they believe it will disrupt their work or cause more harm than good.

Behavioral Resistance: Behavioral resistance is often driven by a lack of skills, resources, or support. Employees may resist change because they don't have the skills or resources to adapt to new processes or systems. They may also feel unsupported or undervalued by leadership, which can lead to resistance.

Political Resistance: Political resistance is often driven by power struggles and competing interests. Employees may resist change because they feel it threatens their power or influence within the organization. They may also resist change because they see it as benefiting a particular group or individual over others.

Cultural Resistance: Cultural resistance is often driven by deeply ingrained beliefs and values within an organization. Employees may resist change because it conflicts with the organization's culture or identity. They may also resist change because they fear it will undermine the values and beliefs that have made the organization successful.

Understanding these types of resistance to change can help leaders develop targeted strategies to overcome them. By acknowledging and addressing employees' concerns and providing them with the support and resources they need to adapt to change, leaders can help their organizations successfully navigate even the most difficult transitions.

1.4 Impact of resistance to change on the organization

Resistance to change can have a significant impact on an organization. When employees resist change, it can lead to decreased morale, increased turnover, decreased productivity, and ultimately, decreased profitability.

One of the main impacts of resistance to change is that it slows down the implementation of new initiatives. When employees are resistant to change, they may drag their feet, procrastinate, or even actively work against the change. This can result in delays, missed deadlines, and increased costs.

Resistance to change can also result in decreased morale among employees. When employees feel that their voices are not being heard and that their concerns are not being taken into account, they may become disengaged and apathetic. This can lead to decreased motivation, decreased productivity, and increased absenteeism and turnover.

Additionally, resistance to change can have a negative impact on the organization's reputation. If the organization is seen as being resistant to change, it may be viewed as being outdated, behind the times, or unwilling to innovate. This can make it difficult to attract and retain top talent, as well as to maintain a competitive edge in the market.

Finally, resistance to change can have a significant financial impact on the organization. If the change is necessary to improve efficiency, reduce costs, or increase revenue, resistance to change can result in missed opportunities for growth and profitability. It can also result in increased costs due to delays, rework, and the need for additional resources to implement the change.

Overall, it is essential for leaders to address resistance to change proactively and to take steps to minimize its impact on the organization. This requires effective communication, strong leadership, and a willingness to listen to employees' concerns and address them appropriately. By doing so, organizations can minimize the negative impact of resistance to change and successfully implement new initiatives that drive growth and success.

Strategies to Overcome Resistance to Change

Resistance to change is inevitable in any organization, and leaders need to have strategies to overcome it. Below are some strategies that can be used to overcome resistance to change:

Communication: One of the most effective strategies for overcoming resistance to change is communication. Leaders need to communicate with the employees about the change and the reasons for it. Communication should be done early and often, and the message should be clear and consistent. The employees need to understand the benefits of the change and how it will affect their work.

Participation: Employees are more likely to accept change if they are involved in the process. Leaders can involve employees in the planning and implementation of the change. This will give them a sense of ownership and make them more committed to the change.

Education and Training: Resistance to change can also be due to a lack of knowledge or skills. Leaders can provide education and training to the employees to help them understand the change and how to adapt to it.

Incentives: Leaders can also use incentives to overcome resistance to change. Incentives can be in the form of bonuses, promotions, or recognition. This will motivate the employees to accept the change and work towards the new goals.

Addressing Concerns: Leaders should also address the concerns of the employees. Employees may have concerns about how the change will affect their job security, workload, or job satisfaction. Leaders need to listen to their concerns and address them to reduce resistance to change.

Leading by Example: Leaders need to lead by example and show their commitment to the change. They need to demonstrate the benefits of the change and how it will improve the organization.

Continuous Evaluation: Finally, leaders need to continuously evaluate the change and its impact on the organization. They need to monitor the progress of the change and make adjustments if necessary. This will help to ensure that the change is successful and that resistance to change is minimized.

In conclusion, resistance to change is a natural part of any organization, and leaders need to have strategies to overcome it. Communication, participation, education and training, incentives, addressing concerns, leading by example, and continuous evaluation are some of the strategies that can be used to overcome resistance to change. By implementing these strategies, leaders can help their organization to adapt to change and stay competitive in the marketplace.

2.1 Effective communication

One of the most important strategies to overcome resistance to change is effective communication. Communication is key in helping individuals understand why change is necessary, what the change will entail, and how it will affect them. Communication must be clear, concise, and honest to be effective in overcoming resistance to change.

Leaders must communicate early and often with employees about the change, including why it is necessary and what the expected outcomes are. They must also explain how the change will be implemented and what the impact will be on individuals, teams, and the organization as a whole. It is important to address concerns and questions that employees may have about the change to avoid misunderstandings and resistance.

Communication should also be tailored to the audience. Different groups may have different concerns or perspectives on the change, so it is important to address those concerns specifically. For example, employees who have been with the organization for a long time may be concerned about how the change will affect their job security or the company culture, while newer employees may be more concerned about how the change will affect their day-to-day work.

Communication should be two-way, with leaders actively seeking feedback and input from employees. This can help to build trust and engagement, and can also help leaders to identify and address concerns before they become major roadblocks to change. Leaders should create opportunities for employees to ask questions, share concerns, and provide feedback, both in group settings and one-on-one meetings.

In addition to verbal communication, leaders should also use visual aids and other forms of media to help communicate the change. This can include presentations, videos, and infographics that help to illustrate the reasons for the change, the expected outcomes, and how the change will be implemented. This can help employees to better understand and remember the information that is being presented, and can also help to build excitement and engagement around the change.

Finally, it is important for leaders to communicate consistently and regularly throughout the change process. This can help to keep employees informed and engaged, and can also help to build trust and confidence in the change. Regular updates can also help leaders to identify and address any concerns or issues that arise throughout the process, before they become major obstacles to change.

In conclusion, effective communication is a critical strategy for overcoming resistance to change. Leaders must communicate early and often with employees, tailoring their messages to different groups and seeking feedback and input throughout the process. By communicating clearly and consistently, leaders can help employees to better understand the change, build trust and engagement, and overcome resistance to change.

2.2 Creating a sense of urgency

Creating a sense of urgency is crucial in overcoming resistance to change. Without a sense of urgency, people are less likely to embrace change, and it can lead to a lack of momentum in implementing the change. Creating a sense of urgency involves communicating the need for change and the consequences of not changing. It is essential to create a compelling reason for change and to communicate this to all stakeholders.

There are several strategies that leaders can use to create a sense of urgency. The following are some of the most effective strategies:

Communicate the need for change: Leaders need to communicate the need for change and why it is essential. They should explain the impact of not changing and the consequences for the organization.

Develop a clear vision: A clear vision can help people understand the direction in which the organization is headed. A vision provides a sense of purpose and a reason to change.

Create a burning platform: Leaders can create a burning platform by highlighting the urgency of the situation. They can do this by identifying the risks and threats that the organization faces and explaining the impact of not changing.

Engage employees: Employees need to be engaged in the change process. Leaders can do this by involving employees in the change process, providing them with the necessary resources and training, and recognizing their contributions.

Demonstrate progress: Demonstrating progress can help build momentum and create a sense of urgency. Leaders should celebrate successes and communicate progress regularly.

Creating a sense of urgency can be challenging, and there are several barriers that leaders may face. The following are some of the most common barriers:

Complacency: Complacency can be a significant barrier to creating a sense of urgency. Leaders must overcome complacency by highlighting the need for change and the risks of not changing.

Fear: Fear is another common barrier to creating a sense of urgency. Leaders need to address fear by providing support and resources to help employees through the change process.

Resistance to change: Resistance to change can also be a barrier to creating a sense of urgency. Leaders need to overcome resistance by engaging employees and communicating the benefits of change.

Lack of resources: A lack of resources can make it challenging to create a sense of urgency. Leaders need to identify the resources required and provide them to employees to ensure that they can embrace the change.

Creating a sense of urgency is essential in overcoming resistance to change. Leaders must communicate the need for change, develop a clear vision, create a burning platform, engage employees, and demonstrate progress. Overcoming barriers to creating a sense of urgency requires addressing complacency, fear, resistance to change, and a lack of resources. By using these strategies, leaders can create a sense of urgency and successfully implement change.

2.3 Involving employees in the change process

Change is a challenging process for organizations, and resistance to change from employees can make it even more challenging. However, one way to overcome this resistance is by involving employees in the change process. When employees feel they have a voice and are valued, they are more likely to accept change and work towards its success.

Here we will explore the benefits of involving employees in the change process and strategies for doing so effectively.

Benefits of Involving Employees in the Change Process

Increased Ownership: When employees are involved in the change process, they are more likely to feel a sense of ownership over the change. This ownership can lead to increased motivation and commitment to the success of the change.

Enhanced Buy-In: Involving employees in the change process can also lead to enhanced buy-in. When employees are involved, they are more likely to understand the reasons behind the change and the benefits it can bring to the organization.

Improved Collaboration: When employees are involved in the change process, it can improve collaboration within the organization. Employees from different departments and levels can work together towards a common goal, which can lead to improved teamwork and communication.

Increased Creativity: Involving employees in the change process can also lead to increased creativity. Employees bring their unique perspectives and ideas to the table, which can lead to innovative solutions.

Strategies for Involving Employees in the Change Process

Communication: Communication is key to involving employees in the change process. Leaders must communicate clearly and consistently about the change and its goals. They should also create opportunities for employees to provide feedback and ask questions.

Training: Leaders must provide adequate training to employees to ensure they have the knowledge and skills to implement the change successfully. This training can also help to alleviate any anxiety employees may have about the change.

Employee Involvement: Leaders should involve employees in the planning and implementation of the change. This involvement can be through focus groups, surveys, or task forces. Employees should be encouraged to provide feedback and ideas throughout the process.

Rewards and Recognition: Leaders should recognize and reward employees who contribute to the success of the change. This recognition can be in the form of public praise, bonuses, or promotions. Recognition can motivate employees to continue their involvement in the change process.

Empowerment: Leaders should empower employees to take ownership of the change. They should give employees the resources and authority they need to implement the change successfully. Empowered employees are more likely to be committed to the success of the change.

2.4 Building a coalition of support

One of the most effective ways to overcome resistance to change is to build a coalition of support within the organization. This coalition can be made up of individuals who have a vested interest in the success of the change effort, including managers, key stakeholders, and influential employees.

Building a coalition of support involves identifying individuals who have a stake in the change effort and can act as advocates for the change. These individuals can help to convince others of the benefits of the change and address any concerns or objections that may arise.

To build a coalition of support, it is important to:

Identify key stakeholders: Identify individuals or groups who will be affected by the change and have a stake in its success. These can include managers, employees, customers, and suppliers.

Engage stakeholders in the change process: Involve stakeholders in the planning and implementation of the change. This can help to build buy-in and ensure that their concerns are addressed.

Develop a communication plan: Develop a communication plan to keep stakeholders informed about the change and its progress. This can include regular updates, meetings, and feedback sessions.

Provide training and support: Provide training and support to help stakeholders adjust to the change. This can include training sessions, workshops, and coaching.

Recognize and reward support: Recognize and reward individuals who support the change effort. This can include public recognition, incentives, and promotions.

Building a coalition of support can help to overcome resistance to change by creating a network of advocates who can promote the benefits of the change and address concerns and objections. This can help to build momentum for the change effort and ensure its success.

2.5 Offering incentives and rewards

Incentives and rewards can be a powerful tool to motivate employees to accept and embrace change. Offering incentives and rewards can help create a positive attitude towards the change process and help employees see the benefits of the change. However, it is important to ensure that the incentives and rewards are meaningful and aligned with the desired outcomes.

Incentives can take many forms, including monetary rewards, promotions, recognition, or opportunities for career advancement. When designing incentives, it is important to consider the target audience and their specific needs and motivations. For example, younger employees may be motivated by opportunities for skill development and career growth, while older employees may be more motivated by financial rewards.

Rewards can also take many forms, including public recognition, team outings, or bonuses. Rewards should be designed to encourage positive behavior and support the desired outcomes. For example, rewarding employees for achieving specific milestones or for making significant contributions to the change process can help build momentum and create a sense of accomplishment.

It is important to communicate the incentives and rewards clearly and consistently, and to ensure that they are achievable and fair. Employees should understand how the incentives and rewards are tied to the change process and how they can contribute to achieving the desired outcomes. It is also important to be transparent about the criteria for earning incentives and rewards, and to ensure that they are distributed fairly and consistently.

Offering incentives and rewards can be a powerful tool for overcoming resistance to change. By aligning incentives and rewards with the desired outcomes, organizations can create a sense of motivation and excitement around the change process, and encourage employees to embrace new ways of working.

2.6 Training and development

One of the reasons why people resist change is the fear of the unknown. They may not be comfortable with the new systems, processes, or tools that come with the change. This can lead to anxiety and resistance. One way to overcome this is by providing training and development opportunities.

By providing training, employees can learn new skills, gain new knowledge, and build confidence in their ability to adapt to the change. This can make them more receptive to the change and reduce their resistance.

The training and development can be delivered in various forms such as workshops, online courses, on-the-job training, and mentoring. It should be customized to meet the needs of each individual and should be relevant to the change that is being implemented.

It is essential to communicate the importance of the training to the employees. Explain how it will help them adapt to the change and how it will benefit them in the long run. Providing incentives such as bonuses, promotions, or recognition for completing the training can also motivate employees to participate.

It is also crucial to provide ongoing training and support. This will help employees to continue to build their skills and knowledge and stay up to date with the changes. By investing in the development of employees, organizations can create a culture of continuous learning and growth, which can help them to stay competitive in the long run.

2.7 Addressing concerns and fears

One of the main reasons for resistance to change is the fear of the unknown. When employees are not sure what the change will entail or how it will affect them, they may become anxious and resistant to the idea. It is important for leaders to address these concerns and fears and provide reassurance to employees.

One effective strategy is to provide as much information as possible about the change and its potential impact. Leaders should be transparent about why the change is necessary, what it will entail, and how it will benefit the organization and its employees. They should also be available to answer any questions and address any concerns that employees may have.

In addition to providing information, it is important for leaders to create a supportive environment where employees feel comfortable expressing their concerns and fears. This can involve creating opportunities for open dialogue and feedback, as well as demonstrating empathy and understanding for employees 'concerns.

Another important strategy is to involve employees in the change process. When employees feel like they have a voice in the decision-making process, they are more likely to feel invested in the change and less resistant to it. Leaders should seek input from employees on how the change will affect their work and what support they may need during the transition.

Finally, it is important for leaders to recognize that addressing concerns and fears may be an ongoing process. Even after the change has been implemented, employees may continue to have questions or concerns.

Leaders should remain open to feedback and be prepared to address any issues that arise.

By addressing concerns and fears, leaders can help to reduce resistance to change and create a more supportive and positive environment for employees. This can ultimately lead to a more successful and sustainable change process.

2.8 Making change manageable

One of the most significant barriers to change is the feeling of being overwhelmed. Change can be intimidating and disruptive, especially if it is a significant transformation. To overcome resistance to change, leaders must break down the change into manageable steps. The following strategies can help make change more manageable:

Develop a clear plan: A clear plan can provide employees with a roadmap for the change process. It should outline the specific steps, timelines, and milestones, so employees can see how the change will unfold.

Prioritize changes: Not all changes are equally important, and some may be more urgent than others. By prioritizing changes, leaders can help employees focus on the most critical changes first and make the change process more manageable.

Assign responsibilities: Employees are more likely to be invested in the change process when they have a clear understanding of their role in it. Assigning responsibilities can also help employees see how their efforts contribute to the overall success of the change initiative.

Provide resources: Employees need the necessary resources to make change happen. This includes everything from funding and technology to training and support. By providing employees with the resources they need, leaders can make the change process more manageable and help employees feel empowered to make the necessary changes.

Celebrate milestones: Celebrating milestones can help employees feel a sense of accomplishment and progress, even if the change process is ongoing. Recognizing employee efforts and successes can also help build momentum and maintain a positive attitude toward change.

In conclusion, breaking down change into manageable steps can help overcome resistance to change. By developing a clear plan, prioritizing changes, assigning responsibilities, providing resources, and celebrating milestones, leaders can help make change more manageable and successful.

Techniques for Overcoming Resistance to Change

In addition to the strategies outlined in the previous section, there are several techniques that can be used to help overcome resistance to change.

Education and Communication: One effective technique is to educate employees about the reasons for the change and communicate the benefits of the change. This can help to alleviate fears and concerns about the change and create a better understanding of why it is necessary.

Participation and Involvement: Involving employees in the change process can also help to reduce resistance. This can be done by soliciting their ideas and feedback, and encouraging their participation in the decision-making process. When employees feel like their voices are being heard, they are more likely to feel invested in the change and less resistant to it.

Negotiation and Agreement: Sometimes, resistance can be overcome by negotiating and reaching an agreement with those who are resistant to the change. This can involve making concessions and compromises in order to find a solution that everyone can agree on.

Manipulation and Coercion: While not ideal, there may be situations where manipulation and coercion are necessary in order to overcome resistance to change. This should only be used as a last resort and with caution, as it can create negative feelings and resentment towards the change and those implementing it.

Building Relationships and Trust: Building strong relationships and trust with employees can also help to reduce resistance to change. When employees feel like they can trust their leaders and colleagues, they are more likely to be open to change and less resistant to it.

By using a combination of these techniques, organizations can overcome resistance to change and successfully implement new initiatives. It is important to remember that each situation is unique and requires a tailored approach in order to be successful.

3.1 Education and information sharing

One of the most effective techniques for overcoming resistance to change is to educate and inform employees about the need for change and the benefits that will come from it. Often, resistance to change arises from a lack of understanding or knowledge about the reasons behind the change. Providing education and information can help address these concerns and help employees see the bigger picture.

Education and information sharing can take many forms, including training sessions, workshops, and presentations. It is important to communicate the rationale for the change, the expected outcomes, and how the change will impact the organization and its employees. It is also important to address any misconceptions or misunderstandings that employees may have.

To be effective, education and information sharing should be an ongoing process. This means providing regular updates and opportunities for feedback and questions. It is also important to use multiple channels for communication, including email, newsletters, intranet sites, and social media.

In addition, involving employees in the planning and implementation of the change can help overcome resistance. This can include soliciting feedback and suggestions, involving employees in decision-making, and providing opportunities for employees to participate in the change process. By involving employees in the change process, they are more likely to understand the need for change and be more committed to its success.

3.2 Participation and involvement

One of the most effective techniques for overcoming resistance to change is to involve employees in the change process. When employees are involved in the change process, they are more likely to support the change and feel a sense of ownership and control over the change.
There are several ways to involve employees in the change process, including:

Soliciting input and feedback: Leaders can ask employees for their input and feedback on the proposed change. This can help identify potential concerns and resistance to the change and allow leaders to address these concerns before they become major roadblocks.
Creating cross-functional teams: Leaders can create cross-functional teams to work on the change initiative. This approach can help ensure that all departments and stakeholders are involved in the process, which can increase buy-in and support for the change.
Encouraging employee participation: Leaders can encourage employee participation in the change initiative by creating opportunities for employees to participate in the planning and implementation process. For example, leaders can hold town hall meetings or other forums

where employees can ask questions, provide feedback, and share their concerns.

Providing training and development: Leaders can provide training and development opportunities to help employees develop the skills and knowledge they need to support the change. This can help employees feel more confident and prepared to deal with the change.

Celebrating success: Leaders can celebrate the success of the change initiative and recognize the contributions of employees who were involved in the process. This can help create a sense of pride and ownership among employees and encourage them to continue supporting the change.

By involving employees in the change process, leaders can help overcome resistance to change and create a culture that is more open to change and innovation.

3.3 Facilitation and support

Another effective technique for overcoming resistance to change is through facilitation and support. This involves providing employees with the necessary resources, training, and guidance to help them adapt to the changes. One way to provide support is by offering training programs or workshops to help employees learn new skills or procedures required by the change. This can help alleviate any fears or anxieties employees may have about their ability to perform their job effectively in the new environment.

Another way to provide support is by assigning mentors or coaches to employees who are struggling with the change. These mentors or coaches can provide guidance, advice, and support as employees adjust to the new way of doing things.

It is also important to provide ongoing support and feedback to employees throughout the change process. This can involve regular check-ins with employees to see how they are adapting and addressing any concerns or issues that arise.

By providing facilitation and support, employees are more likely to feel valued and supported throughout the change process. This can help to reduce resistance and increase acceptance of the change.

3.4 Negotiation and compromise

Negotiation and compromise can be effective techniques for overcoming resistance to change, particularly when the resistance is due to conflicts of interest or different perspectives. Negotiation involves a discussion between the parties involved in the change process to find a mutually acceptable solution. Compromise, on the other hand, involves each party giving up something in order to reach a solution that is acceptable to all.

When using negotiation and compromise to overcome resistance to change, it is important to identify the underlying concerns and interests of the parties involved. This can involve active listening and open communication to understand the perspectives of others. It may also involve creative problem-solving to find solutions that meet the needs of all parties involved.

One important aspect of negotiation and compromise is the need to build trust and rapport with the parties involved. This can be achieved by being transparent, honest, and respectful throughout the negotiation process. It may also involve acknowledging and validating the concerns and perspectives of others, even if they differ from your own.

Another key aspect of negotiation and compromise is the need to remain flexible and open to alternative solutions. This may involve being willing to give up certain aspects of the proposed change in order to reach a compromise that is acceptable to all parties involved.

Overall, negotiation and compromise can be powerful tools for overcoming resistance to change. By building trust and rapport with others, identifying underlying concerns and interests, and remaining flexible and open to alternative solutions, it is possible to find mutually acceptable solutions that can help to move the change process forward.

3.5 Coercion and force

While coercion and force may be effective in some situations, they should be used only as a last resort when all other strategies have failed. These tactics involve using power to make people comply with the changes being implemented, which can lead to resentment and resistance in the long run.

Coercion involves the use of threats and intimidation to make people comply with the change. For example, a manager may threaten to fire an employee who refuses to adopt a new system. Force involves physically imposing the change on people, such as using security to remove employees who are protesting.

Using coercion and force to implement change can result in negative consequences, such as low morale, decreased motivation, and high turnover rates. Employees may comply with the change, but they may do so only because they fear the consequences of not complying.

It is important for leaders to avoid using coercion and force whenever possible and to focus on strategies that promote engagement, involvement, and support from employees. By doing so, leaders can create a more positive and productive work environment that encourages employees to embrace change and work together to achieve common goals.

Addressing Resistance to Change in Different Contexts

Addressing resistance to change can vary depending on the context and situation in which the change is taking place. Here are some strategies to consider for different contexts:

Addressing Resistance in a Traditional Organization: In a traditional organization, change can be met with resistance due to deeply ingrained beliefs and values. To address resistance in this context, it is important to start by gaining the support of key stakeholders who have a strong influence on others in the organization. These stakeholders can help to communicate the vision and benefits of the change, and to encourage others to support it. It can also be helpful to involve employees in the change process, providing opportunities for feedback and input.

Addressing Resistance in a Tech-Driven Organization: In a tech-driven organization, resistance to change can come from employees who are used to a particular technology or software. In this context, it is important to communicate the benefits of the new technology, how it can improve their work processes, and how it aligns with the organization's goals. It can also be helpful to provide training and support to employees to ensure they feel confident using the new technology.

Addressing Resistance in a Diverse Organization: In a diverse organization, resistance to change can stem from cultural differences, language barriers, or different ways of thinking. To address resistance in this context, it is important to create a safe and inclusive environment where everyone feels valued and heard. This can involve providing opportunities for open communication and feedback, and making an effort to understand and respect different cultural perspectives.

Addressing Resistance in a Fast-Paced Startup: In a fast-paced startup, resistance to change can come from employees who are used to moving quickly and making decisions on the fly. In this context, it is important to communicate the vision and benefits of the change in a way that aligns with the startup's fast-paced culture. Providing clear goals and timelines can also help to create a sense of urgency and motivate employees to support the change.

Addressing Resistance in a Non-Profit Organization: In a non-profit organization, resistance to change can come from employees who are deeply committed to the organization's mission and values. To address resistance in this context, it is important to communicate how the change aligns with the organization's mission and values, and how it can help to further the organization's impact. Providing opportunities for employee feedback and input can also help to ensure that the change aligns with the organization's core values.

In all contexts, it is important to listen to employee concerns and to address them in a respectful and empathetic way. By acknowledging and addressing resistance, organizations can create a sense of trust and collaboration, and work towards a successful change outcome.

One of the keys to addressing resistance to change in a global context is to be sensitive to cultural differences. Different cultures may have different attitudes towards change, and what works in one culture may not work in another. For example, some cultures may place a higher value on tradition and stability, while others may be more open to experimentation and innovation.

To address these cultural differences, it is important to involve employees from different cultural backgrounds in the change process. This can help to ensure that the change is perceived as relevant and meaningful to everyone involved. It can also help to identify cultural barriers that may need to be addressed, such as language barriers or differences in communication styles.

Another important factor to consider in a global context is geographic distance. In organizations with operations in multiple locations, it can be challenging to ensure that everyone is on the same page when it comes to change. One strategy to address this challenge is to use technology to facilitate communication and collaboration. For example, video conferencing and online collaboration tools can help to bridge the gap between geographically dispersed teams.

Finally, it is important to recognize that change can be especially challenging in a global context due to language barriers. When introducing change, it is important to communicate clearly and concisely, and to ensure that everyone understands the goals and objectives of the change. This may require translation services or the use of interpreters to ensure that everyone is on the same page.

In conclusion, addressing resistance to change in a global context requires sensitivity to cultural differences, effective communication and collaboration, and a willingness to adapt to the unique challenges of a global organization. By addressing these challenges head-on, organizations can successfully implement change and drive growth and innovation across their global operations.

Addressing resistance to change in a diverse workplace In today's workplace, diversity is becoming increasingly important. Companies are recognizing that having a diverse workforce can lead to a more innovative and productive environment. However, with diversity comes the potential for resistance to change. Different groups of people may have different perspectives, experiences, and values that affect how they perceive change.

To address resistance to change in a diverse workplace, it is essential to consider the following strategies:

Embrace Diversity: It is important to embrace the differences in people and recognize that different perspectives can lead to a better outcome. When implementing change, it is important to consider how it will impact different groups of people and communicate in a way that is inclusive of all.

Create a Culture of Inclusion: Creating a culture of inclusion helps to build trust and respect between different groups of people. This can be achieved through training, mentoring, and other programs that promote diversity and inclusivity.

Listen to Employees: Listening to employees and understanding their concerns is an essential part of addressing resistance to change. This involves creating open lines of communication, actively seeking feedback, and addressing concerns in a timely manner.

Involve Employees in the Change Process: Involving employees in the change process can help to create ownership and buy-in. This can be achieved through brainstorming sessions, focus groups, and other activities that encourage participation.

Provide Support: Providing support to employees during the change process is essential. This can include providing training and development opportunities, offering coaching and mentoring, and providing resources that help employees adapt to the change.

By implementing these strategies, organizations can address resistance to change in a diverse workplace and create a culture that embraces differences and promotes inclusion.

Addressing resistance to change in a crisis situation In a crisis situation, such as a financial downturn or a global pandemic, organizations may need to implement changes quickly to adapt to the new circumstances. However, employees may be resistant to change during a crisis due to heightened stress and uncertainty.

One strategy for addressing resistance to change during a crisis is to communicate clearly and frequently with employees. Leaders should provide regular updates on the situation and how the organization is responding, as well as explain the rationale for any changes being made.

This can help to reduce uncertainty and build trust with employees.

Another strategy is to involve employees in the change process as much as possible. This can include soliciting feedback and ideas from employees, as well as involving them in the planning and implementation of changes. By involving employees in the change process, leaders can help to build buy-in and ownership for the changes being made.

In a crisis situation, it may also be necessary to provide additional support to employees. This can include resources such as counseling or mental health services, as well as training and development opportunities to help employees adapt to new roles or processes.

Finally, leaders should be prepared to make adjustments and revisions to their plans as needed. During a crisis, circumstances can change quickly, and it may be necessary to pivot or make changes to the initial plan. By remaining flexible and adaptable, leaders can help to address resistance to change and ensure the organization is able to navigate the crisis successfully.

4.4 Addressing resistance to change in a digital transformation

Digital transformation involves the integration of digital technology into all areas of an organization, leading to fundamental changes in how it operates and delivers value to customers. The fast pace and constant change of digital transformation can lead to significant resistance from employees who are comfortable with the status quo. Here are some strategies to overcome resistance to change in a digital transformation:

Communicate the benefits: Leaders need to communicate the benefits of digital transformation to employees. This includes explaining how digital transformation can improve efficiency, customer experience, and employee experience. Leaders need to make sure that employees understand the importance of digital transformation and how it can positively impact the organization.

Provide training: One of the main reasons for resistance to digital transformation is lack of knowledge and skills. Leaders should provide training to employees to develop their digital skills and improve their knowledge of new technologies. This will help to build their confidence and reduce resistance.

Involve employees in the process: Employees who are involved in the process of digital transformation are more likely to support the change. Leaders should involve employees in the decision-making process and give them a voice in how the change is implemented. This will help to reduce resistance and increase engagement.

Address concerns: Employees may have concerns about the impact of digital transformation on their jobs, job security, and work-life balance. Leaders should address these concerns and provide reassurance where possible. They should also provide support to employees who may be struggling to adapt to the changes.

Celebrate successes: Leaders should celebrate the successes of digital transformation and recognize the contributions of employees. This will help to build morale and create a positive culture around change.

Provide support: Leaders should provide support to employees who are struggling with the change. This could involve providing additional training or coaching, or providing access to resources that can help employees adapt to the changes.

In conclusion, resistance to change in a digital transformation can be overcome by communicating the benefits, providing training, involving employees in the process, addressing concerns, celebrating successes, and providing support. By taking these steps, leaders can create a positive culture around change and ensure that the organization is well positioned for the future.

Conclusion

In conclusion, resistance to change is a natural response that can arise when organizations attempt to introduce new initiatives. It is important to understand the reasons for resistance to change, which may include fear of the unknown, lack of trust, and perception of loss. However, there are various strategies and techniques that can be employed to overcome resistance to change, including effective communication, creating a sense of urgency, involving employees in the change process, building a coalition of support, offering incentives and rewards, training and development, addressing concerns and fears, and making change manageable.

It is also essential to recognize that different contexts may require unique approaches to address resistance to change. In a global context, for example, cultural differences may affect the acceptance of change, while in a diverse workplace, it is essential to consider how changes may impact different groups. In a crisis situation, quick action may be necessary, but communication and transparency are key to ensuring buy-in. Finally, in a digital transformation, the rapid pace of change requires an agile approach that empowers teams to adapt to rapidly changing circumstances.

By understanding the reasons for resistance to change and implementing effective strategies and techniques, organizations can successfully navigate change initiatives and achieve their desired outcomes.

9.

BUILDING AGILE TEAMS: ADAPTING TO RAPIDLY CHANGING CIRCUMSTANCES

In today's rapidly changing business environment, the ability to adapt quickly is crucial to success. Building agile teams that can respond quickly and effectively to changing circumstances is essential for any organization. This chapter will explore the key principles of building agile teams and offer strategies for creating a culture of agility within your organization.

Understanding Agile Teams

Agile teams are characterized by their ability to respond quickly and effectively to changing circumstances. They are typically made up of cross-functional members who work collaboratively to achieve a common goal. Agile teams are also known for their flexibility, adaptability, and ability to embrace change.

Key Principles of Agile Teams

To build an agile team, it is important to understand the key principles that guide their work. These principles include:

Customer-focused: Agile teams prioritize the needs and expectations of their customers. They work closely with customers to understand their needs, gather feedback, and make changes as necessary.

Iterative and incremental: Agile teams work in short sprints, with each sprint focused on delivering a specific set of features or functionality. The team then gathers feedback, makes any necessary changes, and moves on to the next sprint.

Collaborative: Agile teams work collaboratively, with team members from different departments and disciplines working together towards a common goal. Communication is open and transparent, and team members are encouraged to share ideas and feedback.

Continuous improvement: Agile teams are always looking for ways to improve their processes and deliverables. They regularly review their work, identify areas for improvement, and make changes as necessary.

Strategies for Building Agile Teams

To build agile teams, it is important to focus on strategies that support the key principles of agility. These strategies include:

Hiring for agility: When building a team, look for individuals who are comfortable with change, adaptable, and able to work collaboratively.

Creating a culture of agility: Leaders must create a culture that supports agility. This involves being open to change, encouraging experimentation, and embracing failure as an opportunity to learn.

Establishing clear goals: Agile teams need clear goals and objectives to guide their work. These goals should be specific, measurable, achievable, relevant, and time-bound.

Fostering collaboration: Agile teams rely on collaboration to be successful. Leaders should encourage open communication, create opportunities for team members to work together, and recognize and reward collaborative efforts.

Emphasizing continuous learning: Agile teams must be committed to continuous learning and improvement. Leaders should encourage team members to seek out new knowledge and skills, provide opportunities for training and development, and create a culture that values learning.

Overcoming Challenges in Building Agile Teams

Building agile teams is not without its challenges. Some of the common challenges include:

Resistance to change: Some team members may be resistant to change, which can impede progress and hinder agility. Leaders should address this resistance head-on, emphasizing the benefits of agility and the need for change.

Lack of trust: Agile teams require a high level of trust among team members. Leaders should work to build trust by promoting open communication, encouraging collaboration, and fostering a culture of transparency.

Siloed thinking: Siloed thinking can be a major barrier to agility. Leaders should encourage cross-functional collaboration and create opportunities for team members to work outside of their comfort zones.

Ineffective communication: Effective communication is crucial for agile teams. Leaders should establish clear channels of communication, encourage open dialogue, and ensure that all team members are kept informed and up-to-date.

Understanding Agile Teams

Agile teams are groups of individuals who work together to accomplish a common goal while embracing the principles of agility. An agile team is typically small, cross-functional, and self-organizing, with a focus on delivering value to the customer in a fast, iterative manner. The agile approach emphasizes collaboration, flexibility, and adaptability, with a willingness to experiment and learn from failure.

Agile teams are particularly well-suited to environments that require rapid adaptation to changing circumstances. This can include industries that are subject to frequent disruption or innovation, as well as organizations that are seeking to increase their speed and responsiveness to customer needs.

The agile methodology is often associated with software development, but it has been successfully applied in a wide range of industries, including manufacturing, healthcare, and finance. In recent years, the agile approach has gained popularity as a means of improving organizational performance, fostering innovation, and driving competitive advantage.

Key Principles of Agile Teams

Agile teams are designed to operate in an environment of rapid change, with the ability to quickly adapt to new circumstances, iterate on feedback, and continuously improve. This requires a unique set of principles and practices to be in place.

Here are some of the key principles of Agile teams:

Collaboration: Agile teams work together in a collaborative environment. Team members communicate frequently and openly, sharing ideas and feedback to ensure that the team is moving in the right direction.

Iterative and incremental delivery: Agile teams deliver working software in small, incremental pieces, with each piece adding value to the overall product. This approach allows for faster delivery and feedback, and helps the team to adapt to changing requirements.

Self-organization: Agile teams are self-organizing, meaning that they have the authority and responsibility to make decisions and determine how work is done. This allows for more flexibility and responsiveness to changing circumstances.

Continuous improvement: Agile teams continuously evaluate their processes and seek to improve their performance. This requires a culture of experimentation, where team members are encouraged to try new things and learn from their mistakes.

Customer focus: Agile teams are focused on delivering value to the customer. This means that they prioritize the features and functionality that are most important to the customer, and are willing to make changes based on customer feedback.

By following these principles, Agile teams are able to create a culture of adaptability and innovation, where they can quickly respond to changing circumstances and deliver value to their customers.

2.1 Customer-focused

One of the key principles of Agile teams is to be customer-focused. Agile teams are built to provide value to the customer by delivering solutions that meet their needs. They prioritize the customer's requirements and feedback throughout the development process, ensuring that the end product is tailored to their specific needs.

To achieve customer-focused development, Agile teams often use techniques such as user stories, which capture the user's perspective of what they need the solution to do. User stories help Agile teams to stay focused on delivering solutions that meet the customer's needs rather than getting caught up in technical details that may not be relevant to the customer.

Agile teams also prioritize customer feedback throughout the development process. They use techniques such as continuous integration and delivery to get feedback from the customer early and often, allowing them to make adjustments to the solution as needed. This ensures that the solution is always aligned with the customer's needs and expectations.

By focusing on the customer, Agile teams are able to build solutions that provide real value, resulting in higher customer satisfaction and increased business success.

2.2 Iterative and incremental

The second key principle of Agile teams is being iterative and incremental. Agile teams work in short cycles or iterations, with each iteration building upon the previous one. The team delivers a functional product or feature at the end of each iteration, which is then reviewed and tested by the customer. The customer provides feedback, which is used to refine and improve the product in the next iteration.

This approach enables the team to respond to changing requirements and priorities quickly. It also ensures that the team is delivering value to the customer throughout the project, rather than at the end. This helps to minimize the risk of the project being cancelled or delayed due to changing priorities or requirements.

2.3 Collaborative

Collaboration is an essential principle of agile teams. Agile teams prioritize cooperation and teamwork to achieve shared goals. Team members work together closely, share their knowledge and skills, and continuously communicate with each other to ensure that everyone is on the same page. They collaborate on all aspects of the project, including planning, design, development, testing, and delivery.

To facilitate collaboration, agile teams often use agile methodologies such as Scrum, Kanban, or Lean. These methodologies emphasize teamwork, transparency, and flexibility. They provide a framework for collaboration and communication and help team members to work together more effectively.

Agile teams also promote a culture of open communication and feedback. They encourage team members to speak up and share their ideas and concerns, and they value constructive criticism and continuous improvement. By fostering a culture of collaboration and open communication, agile teams create a supportive and productive work environment that enables them to adapt to changing circumstances quickly.

2.4 Continuous Improvement

Continuous improvement is a key principle of agile teams. It refers to the ongoing process of making incremental improvements to products, processes, and systems to enhance their quality, efficiency, and effectiveness. Agile teams believe that there is always room for improvement and that the best way to achieve this is through an iterative and incremental approach.

Continuous improvement is a proactive approach that involves identifying areas that can be improved and then taking steps to make those improvements. Agile teams regularly review their processes and seek feedback from customers and stakeholders to identify areas for improvement. They then make changes to their processes and systems based on this feedback to ensure that they are always delivering value to their customers.

Continuous improvement is not a one-time activity but rather an ongoing process. Agile teams understand that the needs and expectations of their customers and stakeholders are constantly evolving, and they need to continuously adapt and improve to meet these changing needs. They embrace change and view it as an opportunity to improve rather than a hindrance.

Continuous improvement is also about fostering a culture of learning and experimentation. Agile teams encourage their members to take risks, try new things, and learn from their mistakes. They view failures as learning opportunities and use them to make improvements to their products and processes.

In summary, continuous improvement is a key principle of agile teams. It involves an ongoing process of making incremental improvements to products, processes, and systems to enhance their quality, efficiency, and effectiveness. Agile teams embrace change and view it as an opportunity to improve rather than a hindrance. They foster a culture of learning and experimentation and view failures as learning opportunities.

Strategies for Building Agile Teams

Building an agile team requires a shift in mindset and approach. It requires a commitment to creating a culture that is flexible, adaptable, and focused on continuous improvement. Here are some strategies for building agile teams:

3.1 Develop a shared understanding of the goal

Agile teams need a clear and shared understanding of what they are trying to achieve. This means that the team must have a shared understanding of the goals, objectives, and desired outcomes. It is essential to have a clear definition of success and a roadmap for achieving it.

This understanding should be shared with the team and reinforced regularly.

3.2 Foster a collaborative environment

Agile teams work collaboratively, and building a collaborative environment is essential. The team should have open and transparent communication channels, and all team members should feel comfortable sharing their ideas and opinions. Building a collaborative environment also means creating a culture of trust, where team members can depend on one another and feel safe sharing their vulnerabilities.

3.3 Encourage experimentation and risk-taking

Agile teams need to be comfortable with experimentation and risk-taking. It is essential to create an environment where team members feel free to try new things and make mistakes. This means encouraging a culture of learning and growth, where failures are viewed as opportunities to learn and improve.

3.4 Emphasize continuous improvement

Continuous improvement is a fundamental principle of agile teams. This means that the team is always looking for ways to improve processes, products, and services. It is important to create a culture where continuous improvement is valued, and team members are encouraged to identify areas for improvement and implement changes.

3.5 Build cross-functional teams

Agile teams are cross-functional, meaning that they include individuals with different skills, experiences, and backgrounds. Building cross-functional teams means bringing together people from different departments or functions to work together on a specific project or task. This approach fosters collaboration, innovation, and creativity.

3.6 Provide the necessary tools and resources

Agile teams need the right tools and resources to be effective. This includes access to technology, software, and other resources that support collaboration and communication. It is also essential to provide training and development opportunities to ensure that team members have the skills they need to be successful.

3.7 Support autonomy and accountability

Agile teams work best when team members are given autonomy and are held accountable for their work. This means that team members should be empowered to make decisions and take ownership of their work. At the same time, team members should be held accountable for meeting deadlines and delivering quality work.

In conclusion, building an agile team requires a commitment to creating a culture that is flexible, adaptable, and focused on continuous improvement. By developing a shared understanding of the goal, fostering a collaborative environment, encouraging experimentation and risk-taking, emphasizing continuous improvement, building cross-functional teams, providing the necessary tools and resources, and supporting autonomy and accountability, organizations can create agile teams that are effective, efficient, and successful.

Hiring for Agility

Building an agile team starts with the right people. Organizations need to ensure that they hire individuals who have the potential to work well in a fast-paced, rapidly changing environment. When hiring for agility, organizations need to look beyond an individual's technical skills and focus on their ability to adapt to changing circumstances, their willingness to learn and grow, and their ability to collaborate with others.

To identify potential hires who can thrive in an agile team, organizations should consider the following:

Human Skills: Agility requires effective communication, collaboration, and flexibility. Therefore, organizations should prioritize soft skills during the hiring process. They can look for individuals who are empathetic, open-minded, and comfortable with uncertainty.

Experience: Hiring individuals who have experience working in agile environments can be beneficial, as they are more likely to be familiar with agile principles and practices. However, organizations should also be open to candidates with non-traditional backgrounds, as they may bring fresh perspectives and new ideas.

Learning Mindset: In an agile environment, learning never stops. Organizations should look for individuals who are passionate about learning, experimenting, and trying new things. They should be open to feedback, willing to take risks, and comfortable with failure.

Cultural Fit: Agile teams work collaboratively and emphasize transparency, trust, and respect. To build an effective agile team, organizations should hire individuals who share these values and can work well with others.

Adaptability: Agile teams need to be able to respond quickly to changing circumstances. Therefore, organizations should look for individuals who can adapt to new situations, take on new challenges, and pivot when necessary.

By hiring individuals who possess these traits, organizations can build agile teams that are better equipped to handle the demands of a rapidly changing business environment.

Creating a Culture of Agility

Creating a culture of agility is critical for building and sustaining agile teams. A culture of agility is an environment in which individuals and teams are encouraged to experiment, learn, and adapt quickly to changing circumstances. Here are some strategies for creating a culture of agility:

Emphasize learning and experimentation: Encourage team members to experiment with new approaches and learn from their successes and failures. Celebrate failures as opportunities for learning and growth.
Foster collaboration and cross-functional teams: Encourage cross-functional teams to work together and share knowledge and expertise. Foster a culture of collaboration and trust.
Empower teams: Give teams the authority to make decisions and act on them quickly. Create a culture of empowerment, in which team members are encouraged to take ownership of their work and make decisions.
Encourage innovation: Encourage team members to come up with new ideas and approaches. Create a culture that values innovation and rewards creative thinking.
Provide continuous feedback: Provide regular feedback to team members on their performance and progress. Encourage a culture of continuous improvement, in which team members are always looking for ways to improve their work.
Celebrate successes: Celebrate the successes of agile teams and individuals. Highlight the impact of their work and the value they bring to the organization.

Creating a culture of agility takes time and effort. It requires a commitment from leadership to support and promote agility, and a willingness from team members to embrace change and take risks. But the benefits of a culture of agility are clear: increased innovation, faster time-to-market, and greater resilience in the face of change.

Establishing clear goals

Establishing clear goals is a crucial strategy for building agile teams. Clear goals help team members understand what they are working towards and why it is important. When goals are ambiguous or constantly changing, it can lead to confusion and frustration among team members. This, in turn, can negatively impact team productivity and morale.

To establish clear goals, it is important to involve team members in the goal-setting process. This ensures that everyone has a shared understanding of what the team is working towards and feels invested in achieving those goals. Additionally, goals should be specific, measurable, achievable, relevant, and time-bound (SMART). This makes it easier to track progress and make adjustments as needed.

It is also important to communicate goals frequently and consistently. This helps keep team members focused and motivated, and ensures that everyone is working towards the same objectives. Regular check-ins can help ensure that progress is being made and that any roadblocks are identified and addressed promptly.

Finally, it is important to be flexible and willing to adjust goals as needed. Agile teams are designed to be adaptable, and goals should reflect this. As circumstances change and new information becomes available, goals may need to be revised. By being open to change and willing to adjust goals as needed, agile teams can stay focused and productive, even in rapidly changing circumstances.

Fostering collaboration

One of the key principles of agile teams is collaboration. The success of agile teams depends heavily on how well team members can work together to achieve their goals. Therefore, fostering collaboration is essential for building agile teams.

Here are some strategies for fostering collaboration in agile teams:

Encourage open communication: Encourage team members to communicate openly and honestly with each other. This means creating an environment where people feel comfortable expressing their thoughts and ideas, as well as their concerns and challenges.

Build trust: Trust is critical for collaboration. Team members need to trust each other to deliver on their commitments and to support one another when things get tough. Leaders can build trust by being transparent, honest, and reliable.

Foster a sense of shared ownership: When team members feel a sense of shared ownership over the project, they are more likely to collaborate effectively. This means involving everyone in the planning process and ensuring that everyone has a say in how the project is executed.

Encourage diversity of thought: Agile teams benefit from having team members with different backgrounds, experiences, and perspectives. Encourage team members to share their diverse perspectives and ideas, and be open to feedback and different points of view.

Promote team-building activities: Building strong relationships among team members is critical for effective collaboration. Consider hosting team-building activities, such as retreats, workshops, or social events, to help team members get to know each other better and build stronger relationships.

By fostering collaboration, agile teams can work more effectively together, overcome challenges, and achieve their goals more efficiently.

Emphasizing continuous learning

In order for agile teams to adapt to rapidly changing circumstances, it is essential that team members are constantly learning and developing new skills. This emphasis on continuous learning is a key characteristic of agile teams.

There are several strategies that organizations can use to promote continuous learning within agile teams. One strategy is to provide team members with regular opportunities to attend training sessions and workshops. These sessions can cover a wide range of topics, from technical skills to soft skills such as communication and teamwork.

Another strategy is to encourage team members to pursue their own learning outside of formal training sessions. This can include reading industry publications, attending conferences, or participating in online forums and communities.

Organizations can also promote continuous learning by creating a culture of experimentation and risk-taking. Agile teams are encouraged to try new approaches and techniques, and to learn from their successes and failures. By creating a safe environment for experimentation, organizations can help their teams to stay curious and innovative.

Finally, it is important for organizations to recognize and reward team members who prioritize continuous learning. This can include promotions, bonuses, or other incentives. By placing a high value on learning, organizations can encourage team members to continually develop their skills and knowledge, ultimately contributing to the success of the team and the organization as a whole.

Overcoming Challenges in Building Agile Teams

Building agile teams can be a challenging task, as it requires a significant shift in mindset, culture, and practices. Some of the common challenges in building agile teams include:

Resistance to Change: Resistance to change is a natural response to any significant shift in the way things are done. The traditional hierarchical structures and practices can often create a resistance to change in the organization. It can be challenging to build an agile team within a culture that does not support change.

Lack of Trust: Trust is essential for building an agile team. Without trust, team members may not feel comfortable sharing their opinions and ideas, which can hinder collaboration and innovation.

Communication: Communication is critical in agile teams as they need to work collaboratively and share information frequently. Poor communication can lead to misunderstandings, missed opportunities, and delays in the project.

Time Pressure: Agile teams are expected to deliver results in a shorter time frame. The pressure to meet deadlines can often lead to teams sacrificing quality for speed, which can be detrimental to the project's success.

Resistance to Collaboration: Collaboration is essential for agile teams to work effectively. However, some team members may be resistant to working collaboratively due to personal preferences, past experiences, or cultural differences.

To overcome these challenges, organizations can adopt the following strategies:

Education and Training: Education and training can help team members understand the benefits of agile methodologies and how to work in an agile team effectively. Providing training on effective communication, collaboration, and problem-solving can also help build trust within the team.

Leadership Support: Leadership support is crucial in building an agile team. Leaders should communicate the importance of agile methodologies and create a culture that supports agility.

Team Building Activities: Team building activities can help build trust and collaboration within the team. Activities such as team retreats, workshops, and group problem-solving exercises can help foster a sense of community and shared purpose.

Continuous Feedback: Continuous feedback can help identify issues early and enable teams to make necessary adjustments. Regular retrospectives and check-ins can help teams improve their processes, communication, and collaboration.

Flexibility: Agile teams require flexibility to adapt to changing circumstances. Organizations should be willing to adjust their processes and practices to support their agile teams' needs.

Building agile teams can be a significant undertaking, but with the right strategies and support, organizations can create highly effective and adaptable teams that can thrive in rapidly changing circumstances.

9.1 Resistance to change

One of the biggest challenges in building agile teams is overcoming resistance to change. Agile teams require a shift in mindset and culture, which can be difficult for team members who are used to traditional ways of working. Resistance to change can manifest in many ways, including skepticism, fear of the unknown, and a lack of willingness to learn new skills or adopt new processes.

To overcome resistance to change, it's important to understand the underlying reasons for it. Sometimes, resistance to change is a result of a lack of understanding or knowledge about the benefits of agile methodologies. In other cases, it can be due to a fear of failure or a lack of trust in the team's ability to deliver.

To address resistance to change, it's important to involve team members in the change process from the outset. This can include providing education and training on agile methodologies, as well as soliciting feedback and input from team members. It's also important to establish clear goals and objectives for the team, so that everyone understands what is expected of them and what the team is working towards.

Another effective strategy for overcoming resistance to change is to establish a culture of experimentation and continuous improvement. This can involve creating safe spaces for team members to try out new processes or ideas, without fear of repercussions if things don't go according to plan. It can also involve celebrating successes and learning from failures, to reinforce the idea that change is a necessary part of growth and development.

Ultimately, overcoming resistance to change requires a combination of education, communication, and leadership. By involving team members in the change process and providing them with the support they need to learn and grow, agile teams can overcome resistance to change and build a culture of agility that fosters innovation and continuous improvement.

9.2 Lack of Trust

One of the biggest challenges in building agile teams is establishing trust among team members. In an agile team, members are expected to work collaboratively, share ideas, and take ownership of the work they produce. This requires a high level of trust among team members.

Lack of trust can arise from various factors such as personality clashes, differences in work styles, poor communication, and past experiences. Without trust, team members may hesitate to share their ideas or may not feel comfortable giving and receiving feedback, which can hinder the team's progress.

To overcome the lack of trust, it is important to establish a culture of openness and transparency. This can be achieved by encouraging team members to share their thoughts and ideas openly and providing regular opportunities for feedback. It is also important to establish clear guidelines for communication and collaboration, such as regular check-ins and meetings, to ensure that everyone is on the same page.

Team-building activities and social events can also be effective in building trust and fostering relationships among team members. When team members know and trust each other, they are more likely to collaborate effectively and work towards a common goal.

In addition, it is important for team leaders to lead by example and model the behaviors they expect from their team members. Leaders should be transparent in their decision-making processes and communicate openly with the team. They should also encourage open communication and feedback and be willing to address any issues that arise in a timely and effective manner.

By establishing trust among team members, agile teams can work more effectively and achieve better results.

9.3 Siloed Thinking

One of the biggest challenges in building agile teams is siloed thinking. Silos can be described as isolated units within an organization that do not communicate or collaborate effectively with each other. Siloed thinking can manifest in several ways, such as individual teams working on their tasks without considering how it affects other teams or a lack of cross-functional knowledge-sharing.

Siloed thinking can hinder an organization's ability to be agile as it can lead to slow decision-making and prevent teams from adapting quickly to changing circumstances. To overcome siloed thinking, organizations can take several steps, such as:

Encourage cross-functional collaboration: Encourage collaboration between teams by creating opportunities for team members to interact and work together. Cross-functional collaboration helps to break down barriers and silos.

Promote open communication: Encourage open communication between teams and team members to share knowledge and ideas. This helps to reduce misunderstandings and improve decision-making.

Create a culture of sharing: Establish a culture of knowledge-sharing where team members are encouraged to share their knowledge and expertise with others. This helps to promote a culture of learning and continuous improvement.

Establish clear roles and responsibilities: Clearly define the roles and responsibilities of each team member to avoid confusion and ensure that everyone understands their contribution to the project.

Implement agile methodologies: Implement agile methodologies such as Scrum or Kanban that emphasize collaboration and communication between teams. This helps to ensure that teams are aligned and working towards a common goal.

By implementing these steps, organizations can overcome siloed thinking and build agile teams that are better equipped to respond to changing circumstances and deliver value to their customers.

9.4 Ineffective Communication

Effective communication is crucial for building agile teams. Without clear and frequent communication, team members can become confused, misaligned, and unable to adapt to changing circumstances. Ineffective communication can result in misunderstandings, delays, and mistakes, which can hinder the team's ability to achieve its goals.

One of the biggest challenges in communication is that different team members may have different communication styles or preferences. Some team members may prefer face-to-face communication, while others may prefer email or instant messaging. Some team members may prefer detailed instructions, while others may prefer more general guidance. It's important for agile teams to establish clear communication protocols that work for all team members.

Another challenge in communication is that team members may not feel comfortable expressing their opinions or ideas. This can be particularly true in hierarchical organizations, where team members may feel intimidated by managers or more senior team members. To overcome this challenge, it's important for agile teams to create a safe and supportive environment where all team members feel comfortable expressing their thoughts and ideas.

Finally, communication can be ineffective if team members are not actively listening to each other. Active listening involves not only hearing what the other person is saying but also understanding their perspective and responding in a way that demonstrates that understanding. It's important for agile teams to encourage active listening and to provide training if necessary to help team members develop this skill.

To overcome these challenges, agile teams should prioritize communication and establish clear protocols and expectations for how team members will communicate with each other. Agile teams should also create a safe and supportive environment where all team members feel comfortable expressing their thoughts and ideas, and encourage active listening to ensure that all team members feel heard and understood.

10.

EMERGING TECHNOLOGIES AND THEIR IMPLICATIONS FOR LEADERSHIP

Technology is advancing at an unprecedented pace, and its impact is being felt across all industries and sectors. As a leader, it is important to stay up-to-date with emerging technologies and their implications for your organization. In this chapter, we will discuss some of the emerging technologies that are likely to have the greatest impact on leadership, and what leaders can do to stay ahead of the curve.

Artificial Intelligence

Artificial intelligence (AI) is one of the most transformative technologies of our time. It has the potential to revolutionize everything from healthcare to transportation to finance. As a leader, it is important to understand the implications of AI for your organization. Here are some things to keep in mind:

Automation: AI has the potential to automate many tasks that are currently performed by humans. This could lead to significant cost savings, but it could also lead to job displacement. As a leader, it is important to think about how your organization can prepare for this transition.

Data analysis: AI can analyze vast amounts of data much faster than humans. This can help organizations identify trends and patterns that they might not have otherwise noticed. As a leader, it is important to think about how your organization can leverage this technology to gain a competitive advantage.

Decision-making: AI can help organizations make better decisions by providing insights that might not be apparent to humans. As a leader, it is important to think about how your organization can integrate AI into its decision-making processes.

Blockchain

Blockchain is another emerging technology that has the potential to transform many industries. It is a decentralized ledger that records transactions in a secure and transparent way. Here are some things to keep in mind as a leader:

Security: Blockchain is highly secure because it uses encryption and consensus mechanisms to prevent fraud and unauthorized access. As a leader, it is important to think about how your organization can leverage blockchain to enhance security.

Transparency: Blockchain provides a transparent and immutable record of transactions. This can be particularly useful in industries where trust is important, such as finance and healthcare. As a leader, it is important to think about how your organization can use blockchain to enhance transparency.

Decentralization: Blockchain is a decentralized technology, which means that it does not rely on a central authority to verify transactions. As a leader, it is important to think about how your organization can leverage this technology to reduce costs and increase efficiency.

Internet of Things

The Internet of Things (IoT) is the network of physical devices, vehicles, and other objects that are embedded with sensors, software, and connectivity. Here are some things to keep in mind as a leader:

Data collection: IoT devices can collect vast amounts of data on everything from consumer behavior to equipment performance. As a leader, it is important to think about how your organization can leverage this data to improve operations and customer experiences.

Security: IoT devices are vulnerable to security breaches, which could have serious consequences for your organization. As a leader, it is important to think about how you can secure your IoT devices and protect your organization from cyber threats.

Integration: IoT devices can be integrated with other systems and technologies, such as AI and blockchain. As a leader, it is important to think about how your organization can leverage these integrations to enhance efficiency and effectiveness.

Conclusion

Emerging technologies have the potential to transform industries and change the way we live and work. As a leader, it is important to stay up-to-date with these technologies and their implications for your organization. By understanding the opportunities and challenges presented by emerging technologies, leaders can position their organizations for success in the future.

Artificial Intelligence

Artificial Intelligence (AI) refers to the creation of intelligent machines that can work and learn like human beings. AI is rapidly transforming the world of work, and its impact is likely to increase in the coming years. Leaders need to understand the potential of AI and its implications for their organizations to ensure they are well-positioned to take advantage of its benefits.

AI has the potential to transform a wide range of industries and functions, from customer service to manufacturing, finance, and healthcare. It can automate routine tasks, improve decision-making, and enhance the customer experience. AI technologies such as machine learning and natural language processing can enable organizations to analyze large amounts of data and gain insights that would be impossible for humans to achieve on their own.

However, the rise of AI also raises concerns about its impact on jobs and society. Leaders must consider the ethical implications of AI and take steps to ensure that its deployment does not have unintended negative consequences. They must also develop strategies to address the potential displacement of workers and the need for new skills.

In the context of leadership, AI has significant implications for the role of managers. Leaders need to be able to adapt to the changing landscape and understand how AI can be used to improve organizational performance. They must also be able to manage the implementation of AI systems and ensure that their organizations have the necessary skills and resources to use these technologies effectively.

In summary, AI has the potential to transform the way we work and live, but its impact on jobs and society requires careful consideration. Leaders must develop a deep understanding of AI and its potential applications, as well as the skills and resources required to implement these technologies effectively. By doing so, they can position their organizations to thrive in the age of AI.

1.1 Automation

Automation is a type of artificial intelligence that involves the use of machines and software to perform tasks that are typically done by humans. Automation can take many forms, from simple machines that perform repetitive tasks to more complex systems that can make decisions based on data and other inputs.

One of the key benefits of automation is that it can free up human workers from repetitive, time-consuming tasks, allowing them to focus on more creative and strategic work. For example, automation can be used to perform routine data entry or analysis, allowing human workers to spend more time on developing new ideas or strategies.

However, automation can also have negative implications for leadership. In some cases, automation can lead to job loss, particularly in industries where repetitive tasks are a large part of the work. This can create challenges for leaders who need to manage the impact of automation on their workforce.

Additionally, automation can raise ethical questions around issues such as privacy, security, and bias. For example, automated systems may be biased in their decision-making if they are trained on data that reflects existing biases or inequalities. Leaders must be aware of these potential issues and take steps to address them in order to ensure that their organizations are using automation in a responsible and ethical way.

1.2 Data Analysis

Artificial Intelligence (AI) has given rise to a massive amount of data collection in every aspect of business operations. The importance of data analytics in decision-making has become essential, and AI has given leaders the ability to leverage data analysis tools to make better decisions.

Data analysis refers to the process of inspecting, cleansing, transforming, and odelling data to discover useful information, draw conclusions, and support decision-making. AI technologies are now providing more advanced tools to analyze data faster and more accurately than humans can, and they can identify patterns and trends that might have gone unnoticed.

The implications of AI for leadership are significant. As data analysis becomes more efficient and effective, leaders will need to be able to interpret the data and apply it to their organizations 'operations. This means that leaders will need to be skilled in data analysis and have the ability to identify meaningful insights from the data.

Leaders will also need to understand the ethical implications of data analysis, particularly in the context of privacy and security concerns. As more data is collected, leaders must ensure that they are using it responsibly and in compliance with data protection laws.

Finally, leaders must understand that data analysis is not a substitute for critical thinking or intuition. AI can provide valuable insights, but it cannot replace the human element of decision-making. Leaders must balance the use of AI tools with their own judgment and experience to make informed decisions.

1.3 Decision-making

One of the most significant impacts of artificial intelligence (AI) on leadership is its ability to facilitate decision-making processes. AI-powered decision support systems can process vast amounts of data and provide insights to support more informed and accurate decision-making. This can reduce the time and resources required for decision-making, as well as improve the quality of decisions.

AI can also enable more efficient decision-making processes by automating routine decisions, freeing up leaders to focus on more complex or strategic decisions. This can increase the speed and agility of decision-making, allowing organizations to respond more quickly to changing circumstances.

However, there are also challenges associated with the use of AI in decision-making. One of the key concerns is the potential for bias in AI algorithms, which can result in decisions that unfairly disadvantage certain groups or individuals. It is essential for leaders to carefully consider the ethical implications of AI-powered decision-making and take steps to mitigate bias.

Another challenge is the potential for AI to replace human decision-makers entirely, which can result in a loss of important human judgement and intuition. Leaders must strike a balance between leveraging the benefits of AI-powered decision-making while retaining the value of human decision-making.

Overall, AI has the potential to revolutionize decision-making processes and enable leaders to make more informed and efficient decisions. However, it is important for leaders to carefully consider the potential benefits and challenges associated with the use of AI in decision-making and take appropriate steps to ensure its ethical and effective use.

Blockchain

Blockchain is a decentralized digital ledger technology that has the potential to transform the way businesses operate. It offers a secure and transparent way of recording and verifying transactions, eliminating the need for intermediaries such as banks or brokers. Blockchain is based on a peer-to-peer network of computers that work together to validate and record transactions, creating a permanent and unalterable record.

One of the main advantages of blockchain is that it offers a high degree of security. Once a transaction has been recorded on the blockchain, it is virtually impossible to change or delete. This makes it an attractive technology for applications that require a high level of security, such as financial transactions, identity management, and supply chain management.

Another key benefit of blockchain is its transparency. The technology allows all parties involved in a transaction to see the same information in real-time, which can help to reduce disputes and increase trust. This makes it particularly useful for industries that require transparency, such as food and beverage, where customers want to know the origin and quality of the products they are consuming.

However, implementing blockchain technology can also present challenges. One of the main barriers to adoption is the lack of understanding of the technology and how it can be applied to different industries. Additionally, the technology can be complex and difficult to implement, requiring significant investments in infrastructure and training.

Leaders who want to leverage blockchain technology need to stay informed about the latest developments and applications of the technology. They should also be prepared to invest in the necessary infrastructure and resources, and work closely with industry partners to develop use cases and standards for implementation. Finally, leaders need to be aware of the potential regulatory and legal implications of blockchain technology, particularly in industries that are highly regulated.

2.1 Security

One of the most significant benefits of blockchain technology is its ability to provide secure and tamper-proof transactions. Blockchain achieves this through the use of cryptographic algorithms, which secure data using complex mathematical functions.

When data is added to a blockchain, it is encrypted and linked to the previous block, creating a chain of secure, encrypted data blocks. This process makes it virtually impossible to alter any data in the chain without detection, ensuring that the data is always accurate and secure.

This security feature has implications for leadership in various industries, including finance, healthcare, and supply chain management. For example, blockchain technology can be used to securely store sensitive patient data and ensure that only authorized parties have access to it. In the finance industry, blockchain can be used to secure transactions and reduce the risk of fraud.

However, it is worth noting that while blockchain technology is generally considered to be secure, it is not invulnerable to attack. It is important for leaders to work with experts to ensure that their blockchain implementation is properly secured and maintained to minimize the risk of security breaches.

2.2 Transparency

Another key feature of blockchain technology is transparency. Blockchain is essentially a decentralized ledger system that is publicly accessible, which means that everyone who is part of the network can see every transaction that takes place. This makes the technology very transparent as it creates a tamper-proof record of all transactions that have taken place.

In the context of leadership, this transparency can be leveraged to create more accountability and trust within an organization. By using blockchain technology, leaders can ensure that all transactions and decisions are recorded in a transparent and tamper-proof manner, which can help to prevent fraud and corruption.

For example, in supply chain management, blockchain can be used to create a transparent and auditable record of every step in the production and distribution process. This can help to increase trust between stakeholders and improve the efficiency and security of the supply chain.

However, it is important to note that while blockchain provides a high level of transparency, it does not necessarily guarantee the accuracy or truthfulness of the information that is recorded. Leaders need to ensure that the data that is entered into the blockchain is accurate and reliable in order to fully leverage the benefits of the technology.

2.3 Decentralization

One of the key features of blockchain technology is its ability to operate in a decentralized manner. Unlike traditional systems that rely on a central authority to maintain records and verify transactions, blockchain networks allow for a distributed network of nodes to participate in the verification and validation process.

In a decentralized system, no single entity has control over the network, and each participant has equal access to the system. This creates a more democratic and transparent system that is resistant to manipulation or corruption by any single party.

Decentralization can bring several benefits to an organization or industry. For example, in finance, blockchain technology can facilitate the creation of decentralized financial systems that operate without the need for a central bank or other financial institution. This can potentially reduce fees and transaction costs, and provide more financial access to underserved populations.

Decentralization can also improve the security and reliability of a system by reducing the risk of a single point of failure. In traditional systems, if the central authority were to fail or be compromised, the entire system could be compromised. In a decentralized blockchain network, the failure of a single node or even a group of nodes would not necessarily cause the entire system to fail.

However, decentralization also presents challenges. For example, decentralized networks can be slower and less efficient than centralized systems, particularly as the size of the network grows. Additionally, the lack of a central authority can make it difficult to address disputes or issues that arise within the network. Therefore, organizations must carefully consider the benefits and drawbacks of decentralization before implementing blockchain technology.

Internet of Things

The Internet of Things (IoT) is a system of connected devices, appliances, and machines that can communicate with each other through the internet. IoT has revolutionized the way organizations operate and communicate with each other. IoT devices range from simple sensors to complex systems that control entire manufacturing processes. These devices can collect, analyze, and transmit data in real-time, which enables businesses to make faster and more informed decisions.

IoT has the potential to improve productivity, efficiency, and quality of life. However, it also presents significant challenges for leadership, including:

3.1 Security

One of the biggest challenges with IoT is security. IoT devices can be vulnerable to cyberattacks, and if they are compromised, they can cause significant damage. Cybersecurity risks associated with IoT include data breaches, ransomware attacks, and distributed denial-of-service (DDoS) attacks. Therefore, leaders must implement robust cybersecurity protocols to protect IoT devices and the data they collect.

3.2 Privacy

IoT devices collect a vast amount of data about their users. This data includes personal information, such as names, addresses, and credit card numbers. Therefore, privacy is a significant concern with IoT. Leaders must ensure that they are collecting only the data that they need and that they have clear policies in place regarding how that data will be used.

3.3 Data management

IoT generates vast amounts of data, which can be overwhelming for organizations to manage. Leaders must have a plan in place for collecting, analyzing, and storing IoT data. This plan should include data storage and backup procedures, as well as data analysis tools and techniques.

3.4 Integration

IoT devices often come from different manufacturers and may use different protocols and standards. Therefore, integrating these devices into existing systems can be a significant challenge. Leaders must have a clear plan for integrating IoT devices into their existing infrastructure.

3.5 Training and education

IoT is a rapidly evolving technology, and it requires specialized knowledge and expertise to manage effectively. Therefore, leaders must ensure that their employees are trained on IoT technologies and understand the risks and benefits associated with IoT.

In conclusion, IoT has the potential to transform the way organizations operate and communicate with each other. However, it also presents significant challenges for leadership. Leaders must be aware of these challenges and implement strategies to mitigate them. By doing so, they can take full advantage of the benefits that IoT has to offer while minimizing the risks associated with this emerging technology.

3.6 Data Collection

The Internet of Things (IoT) refers to the interconnection of physical devices, vehicles, buildings, and other objects that are embedded with sensors, software, and network connectivity. These devices collect and exchange data with each other and with their human users, providing new opportunities for organizations to optimize their operations and enhance their customer experiences.

One of the key implications of the IoT for leadership is the massive amounts of data that these devices can generate. IoT devices are capable of collecting a wide range of data, from temperature and humidity readings to customer behavior and preferences. This data can be used to gain insights into how products and services are used, identify opportunities for improvement, and inform decision-making.

However, the sheer volume of data that IoT devices generate can be overwhelming for organizations. Leaders must ensure that they have the infrastructure and tools in place to collect, store, and analyze this data effectively. They must also ensure that they are collecting the right data and using it in ways that are consistent with privacy and security regulations.

Effective leadership in the era of IoT requires a deep understanding of data management and analysis, as well as the ability to identify and prioritize the data that is most valuable to the organization. Leaders must also be skilled in communicating the insights derived from this data to other stakeholders, such as employees, customers, and investors.

3.7 Security

The Internet of Things (IoT) has brought many benefits to both individuals and organizations, but it has also brought new security challenges. IoT devices are often designed to collect and transmit sensitive data, such as personal information or proprietary business data, and they may not always have robust security features built-in. This can make them attractive targets for cybercriminals seeking to steal data or disrupt operations.

One of the key challenges with IoT security is the sheer number of devices involved. With so many devices connected to a network, it can be difficult to identify and manage potential security threats. Additionally, many IoT devices are designed to be low-power and low-cost, which means they may not have the processing power or memory to implement strong security measures.

To address these challenges, organizations must take a proactive approach to IoT security. This includes implementing strong authentication measures to ensure that only authorized users can access the network or the devices connected to it. It also involves implementing strong encryption protocols to protect data in transit and at rest.

Another important consideration is the need for ongoing monitoring and analysis of IoT networks. This can help identify potential security threats before they become major issues, and can help organizations quickly respond to any security incidents that do occur.

Overall, while the IoT offers many potential benefits, it is important to recognize the security risks involved and take steps to address them. By doing so, organizations can ensure that they are able to take full advantage of the benefits of IoT technology while minimizing the risks.

3.8 Integration

Integration is a key aspect of the Internet of Things (IoT). The IoT involves connecting a vast number of devices to a network in order to gather data and communicate with each other. However, integrating these devices into existing systems can be a challenge for organizations.

One challenge with IoT integration is the sheer number of devices involved. Each device has its own software and hardware specifications, which can make it difficult to ensure compatibility with existing systems. In addition, different devices may use different communication protocols, which can complicate the process of integrating them into a single system.

Another challenge with IoT integration is security. The large number of devices connected to the network means that there are many potential entry points for attackers. It is therefore important to ensure that all devices are properly secured and that the network is monitored for any signs of suspicious activity.

To address these challenges, organizations can take a number of steps to ensure successful integration of IoT devices into their systems. One approach is to establish a clear plan for IoT integration that takes into account the unique characteristics of each device and communication protocol. This plan should include a testing phase to ensure compatibility and security.

Another approach is to implement a middleware layer that sits between the devices and the existing systems. This middleware layer can translate between different communication protocols and provide a secure connection between devices and the network.

Finally, it is important to ensure that all devices are properly secured before being integrated into the network. This includes implementing strong passwords, regularly updating firmware and software, and monitoring the network for any signs of suspicious activity.

By addressing these challenges and implementing strategies for successful integration, organizations can fully leverage the power of the Internet of Things and gain valuable insights from the vast amount of data generated by IoT devices.

Conclusion

As new technologies emerge, they bring new challenges and opportunities for leaders in various industries. In this chapter, we have discussed some of the emerging technologies such as artificial intelligence, blockchain, and the Internet of Things, and their implications for leadership.

Artificial intelligence has the potential to automate many tasks, analyze large amounts of data, and assist in decision-making. However, it also raises ethical and privacy concerns. Leaders need to consider the impact of AI on their workforce, their customers, and their organization's values.

Blockchain provides a secure, transparent, and decentralized way to record transactions and share information. Its potential to disrupt various industries is immense, but leaders need to understand how it works and how it can be applied to their business model.

The Internet of Things allows devices to communicate with each other, collect data, and provide valuable insights. However, this also creates security risks and the need for effective data integration. Leaders need to embrace IoT and leverage its potential while mitigating its risks.

In conclusion, as leaders, it is important to stay informed about emerging technologies and their implications for your industry. Leaders who can effectively integrate new technologies into their organization's strategy, culture, and operations can gain a competitive advantage and position their organization for long-term success.

11.

THE FUTURE OF WORK: PREPARING FOR DISRUPTIVE CHANGES

The future of work is being shaped by disruptive technologies, shifting demographics, and evolving work styles. To remain competitive, businesses must prepare for these changes by rethinking their strategies, processes, and organizational structures. In this chapter, we will explore some of the most significant trends that are transforming the workplace and discuss strategies for adapting to the future of work.

The Impact of Disruptive Technologies on the Future of Work

Automation and Artificial Intelligence

The widespread adoption of automation and artificial intelligence (AI) is transforming the workplace, and it's predicted that up to 30% of current jobs may be automated by 2030. As machines and algorithms take over repetitive and routine tasks, workers will need to develop new skills to remain relevant. The ability to work alongside intelligent machines and interpret and manage data will become increasingly important. Organizations must invest in reskilling and upskilling their workforce to ensure that they can thrive in the age of automation and AI.

Blockchain

Blockchain is an emerging technology that has the potential to revolutionize the way we work. It provides a secure, decentralized, and transparent platform for conducting transactions and sharing information. Blockchain technology can enable businesses to streamline their operations, reduce costs, and enhance security. It also has the potential to eliminate intermediaries and create new business models. Organizations should start exploring the potential of blockchain and identifying opportunities to apply it to their business processes.

Internet of Things (IoT)

The Internet of Things (IoT) is the interconnectivity of devices and systems over the internet. IoT devices, such as sensors and wearables, are generating massive amounts of data, which can be leveraged to optimize operations, improve customer experiences, and create new products and services. The widespread adoption of IoT is transforming industries such as healthcare, manufacturing, and transportation. Organizations must adapt to this trend by investing in IoT infrastructure, developing IoT-enabled products and services, and integrating IoT data into their decision-making processes.

Shifting Demographics and Workforce Diversity

Aging Workforce

As the population ages, the workforce is also aging. This demographic shift presents challenges for organizations, such as a shortage of skilled workers and increased healthcare costs. To address these challenges, businesses must adapt their recruiting and retention strategies to attract and retain older workers. They must also invest in training and development programs to enable older workers to acquire new skills and adapt to new technologies.

Diversity and Inclusion

Diversity and inclusion are essential components of the future of work. A diverse and inclusive workforce can bring new perspectives and ideas, leading to innovation and increased productivity. To attract and retain diverse talent, organizations must create an inclusive culture that values and supports diversity. They must also invest in training and development programs that promote diversity and inclusivity.

The Rise of Gig Work and Remote Work

Gig Work

Gig work, also known as the gig economy, is a growing trend in which workers take on short-term, freelance, or contract-based jobs. The rise of gig work has significant implications for organizations, as it requires new approaches to talent management, workforce planning, and employment law. To adapt to this trend, businesses must develop new models for talent acquisition and retention, create flexible work arrangements, and adopt new technologies to manage remote workers.

Section 3.2: Remote Work

Remote work is becoming increasingly popular, driven by advances in technology, changing attitudes towards work-life balance, and the need to reduce office costs. Remote work presents opportunities for organizations to attract and retain talent, reduce costs.

The Impact of Disruptive Technologies on the Future of Work

1.1 Automation and Artificial Intelligence

Automation and artificial intelligence (AI) are rapidly transforming the world of work. Automation involves using technology to perform tasks that were previously done by humans, while AI refers to the ability of machines to perform cognitive tasks that were previously only possible for humans, such as natural language processing and decision-making.

One of the most significant impacts of automation and AI is their ability to replace human workers in certain jobs. This is particularly true for jobs that involve routine or repetitive tasks, such as data entry, assembly line work, and customer service. As these tasks become automated, the need for human workers to perform them decreases, leading to job displacement and a shifting job market.

However, automation and AI also create new job opportunities, particularly in the areas of programming, data analysis, and machine learning. As businesses adopt these technologies, they will require skilled workers who can develop, implement, and maintain them.

Furthermore, automation and AI have the potential to increase productivity and efficiency, freeing up workers to focus on higher-level tasks that require more complex skills and creativity. This shift in job requirements will require workers to develop new skills and competencies in order to remain relevant in the job market.

Overall, while automation and AI may lead to job displacement and changes in the job market, they also offer new opportunities for job creation and increased productivity. It is important for workers and organizations to adapt and evolve in order to stay ahead of these changes and thrive in the future of work.

1.2 Blockchain

Blockchain technology has the potential to revolutionize the future of work by enabling secure and transparent transactions without the need for intermediaries. This technology is based on a distributed ledger that stores transactional data in blocks that are cryptographically linked to form a chain. Each block contains a unique code called a "hash" that acts as a digital fingerprint, making it virtually impossible to alter or delete any transactions.

One of the major advantages of blockchain technology is its potential to eliminate the need for middlemen or intermediaries such as banks, lawyers, or accountants. This could lead to significant cost savings and increased efficiency in various industries. For example, blockchain-based smart contracts could automate the process of executing contracts, ensuring that terms and conditions are automatically enforced, and eliminating the need for lawyers or other intermediaries.

Another advantage of blockchain technology is its potential to enhance security and privacy. The decentralized nature of the technology ensures that data is stored in multiple locations, making it extremely difficult for hackers to manipulate or steal information.

Additionally, blockchain-based systems can ensure data privacy by allowing users to maintain control over their personal information.

However, the adoption of blockchain technology also poses some challenges. One of the biggest challenges is the need for significant investment in infrastructure and training to ensure that employees are equipped with the necessary skills to work with this technology. Additionally, the regulatory environment surrounding blockchain is still evolving, and there is a need for greater clarity on issues such as data protection, intellectual property, and contract law.

Despite these challenges, the potential benefits of blockchain technology are significant, and it is likely to play an increasingly important role in the future of work. Companies that embrace this technology and invest in the necessary infrastructure and training will be well positioned to take advantage of the opportunities presented by blockchain in the years to come.

1.3 Internet of Things (IoT)

The Internet of Things (IoT) refers to a network of physical objects, such as devices, vehicles, and buildings, that are embedded with sensors, software, and other technologies that enable them to collect and exchange data over the internet. This technology has the potential to revolutionize the way we work by enabling us to collect, analyze, and act upon real-time data from a variety of sources.

The use of IoT in the workplace can lead to increased efficiency, productivity, and safety. For example, IoT sensors can be used to monitor the performance of machines and equipment, allowing companies to schedule maintenance before a breakdown occurs. IoT can also help companies optimize their energy consumption by automatically adjusting lighting, heating, and cooling systems based on occupancy and ambient temperature.

However, the widespread adoption of IoT also raises concerns about privacy and security. As more devices are connected to the internet, there is a risk that hackers could gain access to sensitive information or take control of critical systems. To address these concerns, companies must implement robust security measures, such as encryption and authentication protocols, to protect their networks and devices.

Moreover, the implementation of IoT in the workplace requires companies to invest in new technologies and infrastructure, which can be costly and time-consuming. Companies must carefully consider the potential benefits and drawbacks of IoT before making significant investments in this technology.

Overall, the adoption of IoT in the workplace is likely to have a significant impact on the future of work, with both opportunities and challenges. Companies that embrace IoT technology while addressing concerns around privacy and security are likely to benefit from increased efficiency, productivity, and innovation.

Shifting Demographics and Workforce Diversity

The workforce is becoming increasingly diverse in terms of age, gender, ethnicity, and culture. As a result, companies need to create a workplace that can accommodate these differences, promote inclusivity and foster a sense of belonging among all employees.

2.1 Aging Workforce

The global population is aging, and this trend is reflected in the workforce. According to the United Nations, the number of people aged 60 years and above is expected to reach 2.1 billion by 2050, up from 900 million in 2015. This demographic shift has significant implications for the future of work, as older workers bring different skills, experiences, and perspectives to the workforce. However, it also poses several challenges for organizations, such as managing the health and well-being of aging workers, retaining their skills and knowledge, and ensuring a smooth transfer of knowledge to the next generation of workers.

One potential solution is to create age-friendly workplaces that accommodate the needs and preferences of older workers. This could include flexible work arrangements, such as reduced hours, job-sharing, or telecommuting, as well as workplace accommodations, such as ergonomic workstations, larger fonts, and brighter lighting. Additionally, organizations can invest in training and development programs that focus on upskilling and reskilling older workers, as well as mentoring programs that pair older and younger workers to facilitate knowledge transfer.

Another approach is to rethink retirement and provide more opportunities for phased retirement, where older workers gradually reduce their hours or responsibilities over time, rather than abruptly retiring. This allows organizations to retain the valuable skills and knowledge of older workers while also providing them with a more flexible and manageable work schedule.

It is essential to recognize the potential contributions of older workers to the workforce and provide them with the support and resources they need to thrive. Organizations that successfully manage an aging workforce will have a competitive advantage in attracting and retaining talent and fostering a diverse and inclusive workplace.

2.2 Diversity and Inclusion

The workforce of the future will be more diverse than ever before. Inclusion is the active engagement of diverse perspectives, skills, and experiences in the workplace, creating an environment where everyone can contribute to their full potential. A diverse workforce brings a variety of perspectives and experiences, which leads to more creativity, innovation, and better decision-making. The benefits of diversity are clear, but realizing them requires a commitment to inclusion.

To build a truly inclusive workplace, leaders must create an environment where employees feel valued, respected, and supported. They must provide opportunities for employees to share their unique perspectives and ideas, and they must actively seek out and consider diverse opinions when making decisions. This requires a shift in culture, and it requires leaders to challenge their own biases and assumptions.

One way to promote diversity and inclusion is to establish Employee Resource Groups (ERGs). ERGs are voluntary, employee-led groups that represent specific communities or interests within an organization. They provide a platform for employees to connect with others who share similar experiences or backgrounds and offer support and resources to help them succeed in the workplace. ERGs also provide a way for organizations to better understand the needs and perspectives of their diverse workforce and can help leaders identify opportunities to improve diversity and inclusion efforts.

Another important aspect of building a diverse and inclusive workforce is ensuring that all employees have access to the same opportunities for growth and development. This requires a focus on equity, which means recognizing that different employees may have different needs and providing support and resources to address those needs. Leaders must also be intentional about creating a culture of respect and accountability, where bias and discrimination are not tolerated, and employees are held accountable for their actions.

In summary, building a diverse and inclusive workforce is essential for the future of work. It requires a commitment to creating an environment where everyone can contribute to their full potential, and where employees feel valued, respected, and supported. By embracing diversity and inclusion, organizations can harness the power of different perspectives and experiences to drive innovation, creativity, and better decision-making.

The Rise of Gig Work and Remote Work

The traditional model of full-time employment with one employer is changing rapidly. A growing number of people are choosing to work independently as freelancers, contractors, or in the gig economy. At the same time, advances in technology are making remote work more feasible and attractive to both workers and employers. These trends are expected to continue and even accelerate in the coming years, leading to a significant transformation of the workforce.

3.1 Gig Work

The rise of gig work, also known as the gig economy, refers to a labor market characterized by the prevalence of short-term, flexible contracts or freelance work, as opposed to permanent jobs. This trend has been driven by the increasing availability and adoption of online platforms and apps that facilitate direct connections between clients and workers. Gig work has been enabled by the growth of the internet and the ability to work from virtually anywhere with a reliable internet connection.

Gig work has been embraced by many workers who appreciate the flexibility and autonomy it provides, as well as the ability to earn income from multiple sources. Employers have also been attracted to gig work as it offers greater flexibility and cost-effectiveness compared to traditional employment models.

However, the rise of gig work has also raised concerns about job security and the erosion of traditional employment relationships. Many gig workers lack access to traditional employment benefits such as health insurance, retirement plans, and paid time off. The unpredictable nature of gig work can also create financial instability and uncertainty for workers.

In response to these concerns, there has been a growing movement to establish greater protections and benefits for gig workers, including calls for the reclassification of some gig workers as employees rather than independent contractors. However, there is still significant debate over how to balance the flexibility and autonomy of gig work with the need for worker protections and benefits.

Another trend that has contributed to the rise of gig work is the increasing popularity of remote work. Advances in technology have made it possible for many workers to perform their jobs from anywhere with an internet connection, eliminating the need for a physical office space. This has enabled more people to work on a freelance or contract basis, contributing to the growth of the gig economy.

Overall, the rise of gig work represents a significant shift in the way that work is organized and performed. As this trend continues, it will be important for organizations and policymakers to balance the benefits of flexibility and autonomy with the need for worker protections and benefits.

3.2 Remote Work

Remote work, also known as telecommuting, virtual work, or telework, refers to a work arrangement where employees work outside of the traditional office environment, often from home or a remote location. With advancements in technology and communication tools, remote work has become increasingly popular in recent years.

One of the biggest benefits of remote work is the flexibility it provides for both employers and employees. For employers, remote work can lead to cost savings in office space, reduced overhead costs, and access to a wider pool of talent. For employees, remote work can provide a better work-life balance, reduce commuting time and expenses, and increase productivity.

However, remote work also poses unique challenges, such as maintaining communication and collaboration, ensuring data security and privacy, and managing performance and productivity. Leaders must adapt to the changing nature of work and embrace remote work as a viable option to attract and retain top talent.

Effective leadership in a remote work environment requires clear communication, trust-building, and a focus on results rather than hours worked. Leaders must also provide the necessary resources and support for remote employees to ensure they have the tools and technology they need to be successful.

As the trend towards remote work continues to grow, leaders must be prepared to navigate the challenges and opportunities presented by this shift in the way we work.

By embracing remote work and providing the necessary support and guidance, leaders can create a culture of productivity, collaboration, and innovation in a remote work environment.

3.3 Challenges and Opportunities

The rise of gig work and remote work has created both challenges and opportunities for organizations and individuals.

One of the primary challenges is managing a distributed workforce. With remote work, employees may be located in different time zones, making communication and collaboration more difficult. This can also lead to feelings of isolation among team members. Organizations need to provide their remote employees with the tools and resources they need to stay connected and engaged with their colleagues.

Another challenge is maintaining company culture and values in a remote or gig work environment. In a traditional office setting, culture is often built through daily interactions and shared experiences. In a remote or gig work setting, it can be more difficult to create a sense of community and shared purpose. Organizations need to find ways to maintain their culture and values in a remote or gig work environment, such as through virtual team building activities or regular check-ins with remote workers.

However, the rise of gig work and remote work also presents opportunities for organizations and individuals. For organizations, it allows them to access a wider pool of talent and reduce overhead costs associated with maintaining a physical office space. It also enables organizations to be more agile and responsive to changing market conditions.

For individuals, it provides greater flexibility and autonomy over their work schedule and location. It allows them to work on projects that align with their skills and interests, rather than being limited by the job opportunities available in their immediate geographic area.

Overall, the rise of gig work and remote work is transforming the way we work and creating new challenges and opportunities for organizations and individuals. To be successful in this new environment, organizations and individuals must be adaptable, creative, and willing to embrace change.

12.

THE ETHICS OF DIGITAL LEADERSHIP: BALANCING PROFIT AND SOCIAL RESPONSIBILITY

In recent years, businesses have become increasingly reliant on digital technologies to improve efficiency, increase profits, and create new opportunities. However, this reliance on technology has also raised new ethical concerns for leaders and organizations, particularly when it comes to balancing the pursuit of profits with social responsibility.

Understanding Digital Ethics

Defining Digital Ethics

Digital ethics refers to the moral principles and values that guide ethical behavior in the use of digital technologies. It involves considering the potential impact of technology on individuals, society, and the environment, and making decisions that promote the common good.

The Importance of Digital Ethics

As technology continues to shape the way we work and live, it is becoming increasingly important for leaders to consider the ethical implications of their actions. Organizations that fail to consider digital ethics risk harming their reputation, losing customer trust, and facing legal or regulatory penalties.

Key Ethical Issues in Digital Leadership

Data Privacy and Security

Data privacy and security are major concerns in the digital age, particularly as organizations collect and store increasing amounts of personal data. Leaders must take steps to protect sensitive information and ensure that it is used in ways that are ethical and transparent.

Artificial Intelligence and Automation

As organizations increasingly rely on AI and automation to improve efficiency and accuracy, leaders must consider the ethical implications of these technologies. This includes ensuring that these systems are transparent, unbiased, and do not perpetuate discrimination or inequality.

Digital Inclusion and Accessibility

Leaders must consider the impact of digital technologies on access and inclusion, particularly for marginalized communities. This includes ensuring that technology is accessible to people with disabilities and providing training and support for individuals who may be less familiar with these tools.

Strategies for Ethical Digital Leadership

Develop Ethical Guidelines

Leaders should develop clear ethical guidelines for the use of digital technologies within their organizations. These guidelines should be communicated clearly to employees and should provide guidance on key ethical issues such as data privacy and security, digital inclusion and accessibility, and the use of AI and automation.

Foster a Culture of Ethical Behavior

Leaders should work to create a culture of ethical behavior within their organizations. This includes promoting transparency, accountability, and responsibility, and encouraging employees to speak up about ethical concerns.

Invest in Training and Education

Leaders should invest in training and education to ensure that employees have the skills and knowledge needed to make ethical decisions in the use of digital technologies. This includes providing training on data privacy and security, digital inclusion and accessibility, and ethical decision-making.

Conclusion

As digital technologies continue to shape the way we work and live, it is becoming increasingly important for leaders to consider the ethical implications of their actions. By developing clear ethical guidelines, fostering a culture of ethical behavior, and investing in training and education, leaders can ensure that their organizations are well-equipped to navigate the ethical challenges of the digital age.

Understanding Digital Ethics

The rapid growth of digital technology has created an unprecedented level of interconnectedness, generating vast amounts of data that can be processed, analyzed, and used to drive innovation and growth. However, this same technology has also raised new ethical concerns that must be considered by leaders in the digital age. Digital ethics involves examining the moral and ethical implications of using technology and data, particularly in relation to issues such as privacy, security, transparency, and accountability.

As leaders, it is important to understand the ethical implications of digital technology, particularly as it relates to the use of data. In the digital age, data has become a valuable commodity, and the way that companies collect, store, use, and share data can have significant ethical implications. For example, data breaches can compromise the privacy and security of individuals, while the use of data to drive personalized advertising can raise concerns about manipulation and the use of personal information without consent.

In addition, leaders must also consider the potential impact of digital technology on society as a whole. While technology has the potential to drive significant economic growth and improve the quality of life for many individuals, it can also exacerbate existing inequalities and create new ethical challenges. For example, the use of algorithms in hiring and other decision-making processes may perpetuate existing biases, while the increasing use of automation may lead to job displacement and the erosion of workers' rights.

To navigate these ethical challenges, digital leaders must adopt a values-based approach that prioritizes transparency, accountability, and social responsibility. By embracing ethical values and principles, digital leaders can help ensure that technology is used in a way that benefits society as a whole, rather than simply serving the interests of a few.

1.1 Defining Digital Ethics

As the world becomes increasingly digital, the importance of ethical leadership in the digital realm has become more significant. Digital ethics refers to the set of moral principles that govern the behavior of individuals and organizations in the digital space. It involves the responsible and ethical use of digital technologies, data, and information.

Digital ethics encompasses a range of issues, including privacy, data security, intellectual property, and responsible use of social media. It also involves understanding the impact of digital technologies on society and the environment, and considering the ethical implications of technology-related decisions.

The digital era has brought forth new ethical challenges, including the rapid spread of disinformation, the misuse of personal data, and the potential for technology to perpetuate bias and discrimination. Digital ethics aims to address these challenges and ensure that individuals and organizations use technology in a responsible and ethical manner.

1.2 The Importance of Digital Ethics

As technology continues to advance, digital leaders have more power and responsibility than ever before. The decisions made by these leaders can have a significant impact on their organization, employees, customers, and society as a whole. Therefore, it is important for digital leaders to consider the ethical implications of their actions.

The importance of digital ethics can be seen in several areas. For example, privacy is a critical concern in the digital age, and leaders must take steps to protect the personal data of their customers and employees. In addition, the use of artificial intelligence and automation raises questions about the impact on employment and the ethical treatment of workers. Digital leaders must also consider the potential for their technologies to perpetuate biases and discrimination.

Ultimately, digital ethics is about finding the balance between pursuing profits and fulfilling social responsibilities. By taking a thoughtful and ethical approach to leadership, digital leaders can ensure that their organizations are not only successful but also contributing to a better world.

Key Ethical Issues in Digital Leadership

2.1 Data Privacy and Security

In the digital age, data has become a valuable commodity, and the collection and use of personal information has raised concerns about privacy and security. Digital leaders must prioritize data privacy and security to ensure that they are complying with laws and regulations, as well as building trust with their customers and stakeholders.

One aspect of data privacy is the collection and use of personal information. Digital leaders must be transparent about the information they collect, how it is used, and who has access to it. They must also obtain consent from individuals before collecting and using their personal information. This can be achieved through clear and concise privacy policies, opt-in mechanisms, and other tools to give individuals control over their data.

In addition, digital leaders must ensure that data is stored and transmitted securely. This includes implementing appropriate security measures such as encryption, access controls, and regular monitoring and testing of systems. They must also be prepared to respond quickly and effectively to data breaches or other security incidents.

Ultimately, digital leaders must balance the benefits of data collection and use with the rights and expectations of individuals to privacy and security. By prioritizing data privacy and security, they can build trust with their customers and stakeholders, and maintain their reputation and credibility in the digital age.

2.2 Artificial Intelligence and Automation

Artificial Intelligence (AI) and automation are transforming the way businesses operate, and the role of digital leaders is becoming increasingly important in navigating the ethical implications of these technologies.

AI and automation have the potential to streamline operations, improve efficiency, and reduce costs, but they also raise important ethical concerns. For example, the use of AI in hiring and recruitment may perpetuate existing biases, and the automation of certain jobs may lead to significant job losses and social disruption.

Digital leaders must consider the ethical implications of AI and automation in their decision-making processes. They must ensure that these technologies are being used in a responsible and transparent manner, and that they are not perpetuating existing biases or causing harm to individuals or society as a whole.

One key area of concern is the use of AI in decision-making. As AI algorithms become more advanced and sophisticated, there is a risk that they may make decisions that are not only biased but also harmful to individuals or groups. For example, a facial recognition algorithm may incorrectly identify a person as a criminal, leading to their arrest and incarceration. Digital leaders must ensure that these algorithms are transparent and accountable, and that they are not being used to make decisions that are unfair or discriminatory.

Another area of concern is the impact of automation on employment. While automation has the potential to improve productivity and reduce costs, it may also lead to significant job losses and social disruption. Digital leaders must consider the ethical implications of automation on their workforce and take steps to mitigate the impact on employees.

In summary, digital leaders must be aware of the ethical implications of AI and automation and take steps to ensure that these technologies are being used in a responsible and transparent manner. They must consider the impact of these technologies on individuals and society as a whole and take steps to mitigate any negative effects.

2.3 Digital Inclusion and Accessibility

Digital inclusion and accessibility are crucial aspects of digital ethics that leaders must consider. In the digital age, access to technology and the internet is essential for participating in society, accessing information, and achieving economic success. However, not all individuals and communities have equal access to these resources.

Digital inclusion refers to the efforts to ensure that all individuals have access to digital technologies and the skills necessary to use them effectively. This includes addressing issues of affordability, internet connectivity, and digital literacy. For example, a leader might work to provide internet access and training to underserved communities, or to make their products and services more accessible to individuals with disabilities.

Digital accessibility, on the other hand, refers to designing technology and digital products in a way that is accessible to all users, including those with disabilities. This might involve creating websites and apps that are compatible with screen readers or designing products that can be used without requiring fine motor skills. Leaders must prioritize digital accessibility to ensure that all individuals, regardless of ability, can benefit from digital technologies.

In conclusion, digital inclusion and accessibility are essential components of digital ethics that leaders must prioritize. By addressing issues of access and designing products that are accessible to all users, leaders can create a more inclusive and equitable digital world.

Strategies for Ethical Digital Leadership

As digital technologies continue to advance and become increasingly integrated into business operations, ethical leadership becomes more crucial than ever before. Leaders must take responsibility for ensuring that their organizations operate in an ethical and socially responsible manner. Here are some strategies for ethical digital leadership:

3.1 Develop and Communicate Clear Ethical Standards

Leaders should develop and communicate clear ethical standards that guide their organization's behavior and decision-making. This includes establishing a code of ethics that outlines the organization's values and principles, and creating policies and procedures that ensure compliance with relevant laws and regulations. Clear ethical standards provide guidance for employees, stakeholders, and customers, and help build trust and credibility.

In order to foster an ethical digital workplace, it is essential for leaders to establish clear guidelines and policies that outline ethical practices and values. These guidelines should be developed with input from all stakeholders, including employees, customers, and community members, and should be regularly reviewed and updated to ensure they remain relevant and effective. The guidelines should include a code of conduct that outlines expectations for ethical behavior and decision-making, as well as policies and procedures for handling ethical concerns and violations. The code of conduct should cover topics such as data privacy, security, and confidentiality, as well as issues related to discrimination, harassment, and bias.

In addition to developing these guidelines, it is important for leaders to ensure that they are communicated effectively to all members of the organization. This may involve conducting training sessions or workshops to educate employees on the guidelines and their importance, as well as providing ongoing support and resources for ethical decision-making.

Leaders should also model ethical behavior and decision-making themselves, serving as role models for their employees and demonstrating a commitment to upholding the organization's values and ethical principles. This can help to create a culture of ethical behavior throughout the organization and establish a strong foundation for ethical digital leadership.

3.2 Foster a Culture of Ethics and Responsibility

Leaders should foster a culture of ethics and responsibility within their organization. This involves promoting an environment in which ethical behavior is expected and rewarded, and unethical behavior is not tolerated. Leaders should encourage open communication, transparency, and accountability, and should provide employees with the tools and resources they need to make ethical decisions.

Developing ethical guidelines is just the first step towards achieving ethical digital leadership. Leaders must also ensure that these guidelines are effectively communicated and integrated into the organizational culture. This requires a commitment to fostering a culture of ethical behavior, where employees understand the importance of ethical decision-making and are empowered to act on it.

To achieve this, leaders must model ethical behavior themselves and consistently reinforce the importance of ethical decision-making. This includes regularly communicating about ethical guidelines and providing training to employees on how to apply them in their work. Leaders should also establish clear expectations for ethical behavior and hold employees accountable for adhering to them.

Another important aspect of fostering a culture of ethical behavior is creating an environment where employees feel safe to speak up about ethical concerns. This can be achieved through the establishment of anonymous reporting mechanisms, as well as ensuring that there are no negative consequences for speaking up.

In addition, leaders should foster an environment of transparency and accountability. This includes being transparent about how data is collected, used, and shared, as well as regularly reporting on the organization's ethical practices and outcomes.

Ultimately, building a culture of ethical behavior requires a long-term commitment from leaders and a willingness to continuously evaluate and improve ethical practices. By fostering such a culture, organizations can not only ensure that they are operating in an ethical and responsible manner, but also enhance their reputation and build trust with customers and stakeholders.

3.3 Ensure Data Privacy and Security

Leaders must take steps to ensure the privacy and security of their customers' data. This includes implementing robust security measures, such as encryption and firewalls, and regularly reviewing and updating those measures to stay ahead of emerging threats. It also means being transparent about how data is collected, used, and shared, and providing customers with the option to opt out of data collection and sharing.

3.4 Promote Digital Inclusion and Accessibility

Leaders should promote digital inclusion and accessibility within their organizations. This includes ensuring that all employees, customers, and stakeholders have equal access to digital resources and tools, regardless of their race, gender, or disability status. Leaders should also ensure that their digital products and services are designed with accessibility in mind, and should seek input and feedback from diverse groups of people to ensure that their products are inclusive and user-friendly.

3.5 Be Accountable and Transparent

Finally, leaders must be accountable and transparent in their actions and decisions. This means acknowledging and learning from mistakes, and taking responsibility for any negative consequences that may arise from their decisions. It also means being transparent about the organization's goals, values, and operations, and communicating openly with stakeholders about any issues or challenges that may arise.

In conclusion, ethical digital leadership is essential for organizations that seek to balance profit and social responsibility. Leaders must develop and communicate clear ethical standards, foster a culture of ethics and responsibility, ensure data privacy and security, promote digital inclusion and accessibility, and be accountable and transparent in their actions and decisions. By following these strategies, leaders can create an ethical and socially responsible organization that serves the needs of all stakeholders.

3.6 Invest in Training and Education

One of the most effective ways to promote ethical digital leadership is by investing in training and education for employees. This includes providing ongoing training programs that focus on ethical behavior in the digital realm, including the latest policies and best practices for data privacy, security, and transparency. By providing these training programs, leaders can ensure that employees are equipped with the knowledge and skills they need to make ethical decisions in their work.

Leaders can also encourage employees to attend conferences, seminars, and workshops that focus on digital ethics and responsibility. This allows employees to stay up-to-date on the latest trends and challenges in digital ethics, and to learn from experts in the field.

Furthermore, leaders can invest in digital literacy programs to ensure that employees have the necessary skills to navigate digital technologies effectively and responsibly. This can include training in basic digital skills, such as online communication, data management, and security protocols.

Leaders can also consider partnering with educational institutions to develop customized training programs and certifications that address specific ethical challenges in their industry. For example, companies in the healthcare industry may partner with medical schools to provide training programs on the ethical use of patient data.

Overall, investing in training and education is an essential component of promoting ethical digital leadership. By equipping employees with the knowledge and skills they need to navigate the digital landscape responsibly, leaders can create a culture of ethical behavior and ensure that their organizations are well-positioned to meet the challenges of the digital age.

Conclusion

In conclusion, digital ethics is an essential consideration for leaders in the digital age. As businesses increasingly rely on digital technologies, leaders must ensure that their practices prioritize the well-being of all stakeholders, including customers, employees, and society at large. Failure to do so can result in reputational damage, regulatory penalties, and even legal action.

To navigate the complexities of digital ethics, leaders should develop clear guidelines, foster a culture of ethical behavior, and invest in training and education. By doing so, they can build trust with their stakeholders and position themselves as leaders in their industry.

Ultimately, ethical digital leadership is about finding a balance between profit and social responsibility. It requires leaders to make difficult decisions that prioritize the needs of their stakeholders while still driving business growth. With careful consideration and a commitment to ethical behavior, leaders can successfully navigate this balance and build a sustainable and responsible digital future.

13.

CONCLUSION: DEVELOPING A PERSONALIZED APPROACH TO DIGITAL LEADERSHIP

As we have seen throughout this book, digital leadership is a complex and rapidly evolving field that requires a personalized approach. To be a successful digital leader, you must understand the latest digital trends, build and manage agile teams, and balance the competing demands of profit and social responsibility.

To achieve this, you must be willing to constantly learn and adapt, staying up to date on emerging technologies and best practices. You must also prioritize ethics and social responsibility, developing a culture of ethical behavior within your organization and investing in training and education to ensure that your team is equipped to navigate the complex ethical landscape of digital leadership.

At the same time, you must recognize the unique challenges and opportunities presented by your organization and industry, tailoring your approach to meet the specific needs and demands of your team and customers. By taking a personalized approach to digital leadership, you can build a successful and sustainable organization that is prepared to thrive in the digital age.

As you move forward in your digital leadership journey, remember that success is not a destination, but a continuous journey of learning and growth. By embracing this mindset, you can develop the skills and strategies necessary to lead your organization to success in the digital age.

Digital leadership is an evolving field that requires continuous learning and adaptation. As we have seen throughout this guide, there are various disruptive technologies and trends that are shaping the future of work and business. To be effective in this environment, digital leaders must be able to navigate these changes and develop a personalized approach that is in line with their organization's goals and values.

To achieve this, digital leaders should prioritize building a strong foundation of skills and knowledge that will allow them to stay ahead of emerging trends and technologies. This includes developing a deep understanding of data analytics, automation, and artificial intelligence, as well as cultivating strong communication, collaboration, and strategic thinking skills.

In addition, digital leaders must embrace a set of ethical principles that guide their decision-making and actions. This includes prioritizing data privacy and security, fostering a culture of inclusion and accessibility, and investing in training and education to ensure that everyone in their organization is equipped to navigate the complex and rapidly changing digital landscape.

Ultimately, the key to effective digital leadership is a willingness to adapt and evolve, while also staying true to the core values and vision of the organization. By taking a personalized approach that is grounded in a deep understanding of the latest trends and technologies, as well as a commitment to ethical principles, digital leaders can position themselves and their organizations for success in the digital age.

XX.
REFERENCES

Adams, B., & Stewart, K. (2016). Adaptive leadership and technology: Ensuring relevance for future leadership. Journal of Leadership Education, 15(3), 168-178.

Bass, B. M. (1985). Leadership and performance beyond expectations. New York: Free Press.

Bass, B. M., & Avolio, B. J. (1993). Transformational leadership and organizational culture. Public Administration Quarterly, 17(1), 112-121.

Berson, Y., Halevy, N., & Shamir, B. (2012). The elusive benefits of proactive personality for leadership emergence: A multi-follower perspective. Journal of Applied Psychology, 97(2), 445-454.

Burns, J. M. (1978). Leadership. New York: Harper & Row.

Choudhary, A. I., Akhtar, S. A., & Zaheer, A. (2013). Impact of transformational and servant leadership on organizational performance: A comparative analysis. Journal of Business Ethics, 116(2), 433-440.

Conger, J. A., & Kanungo, R. N. (1987). Toward a behavioral theory of charismatic leadership in organizational settings. Academy of Management Review, 12(4), 637-647.

Goleman, D. (1995). Emotional intelligence. New York: Bantam.

Goleman, D., Boyatzis, R. E., & McKee, A. (2002). Primal leadership: Realizing the power of emotional intelligence. Boston: Harvard Business Press.

Hackman, J. R., & Wageman, R. (2007). Asking the right questions about leadership: Discussion and conclusions. American Psychologist, 62(1), 43-47.

Kotter, J. P. (1990). What leaders really do. Harvard Business Review, 68(3), 103-111.

Luthans, F., & Youssef, C. M. (2007). Emerging positive organizational behavior. Journal of Management, 33(3), 321-349.

Mayer, J. D., Salovey, P., & Caruso, D. R. (2004). Emotional intelligence: Theory, findings, and implications. Psychological Inquiry, 15(3), 197-215.

Northouse, P. G. (2015). Leadership: Theory and practice. Thousand Oaks, CA: Sage.

Riggio, R. E. (2008). Introduction to industrial/organizational psychology. Upper Saddle River, NJ: Pearson Prentice Hall.

Yukl, G. (2006). Leadership in organizations (6th ed.). Upper Saddle River, NJ: Pearson/Prentice Hall.

www.ingramcontent.com/pod-product-compliance
Lightning Source LLC
Chambersburg PA
CBHW070540220526
45467CB00003B/1002